THE
FIRST-TIME
MANAGER

FIFTH EDITION

THE
FIRST-TIME
MANAGER

FIFTH EDITION

Loren B. Belker
& Gary S. Topchik

AMACOM

American Management Association

New York • Atlanta • Brussels • Chicago • Mexico City • San Francisco
Shanghai • Tokyo • Toronto • Washington, D. C.

Special discounts on bulk quantities of AMACOM books are available to corporations, professional associations, and other organizations. For details, contact Special Sales Department, AMACOM, a division of American Management Association, 1601 Broadway, New York, NY 10019.
Tel.: 212-903-8316. Fax: 212-903-8083.
Web Site: www.amacombooks.org

This publication is designed to provide accurate and authoritative information in regard to the subject matter covered. It is sold with the understanding that the publisher is not engaged in rendering legal, accounting, or other professional service. If legal advice or other expert assistance is required, the services of a competent professional person should be sought.

Library of Congress Cataloging-in-Publication Data

Belker, Loren B.
    The first-time manager / Loren B. Belker, Gary S. Topchik.—5th ed.
        p.   cm.
        ISBN-10: 0-8144-0821-4
        ISBN-13: 978-0-8144-0821-6
    1. Supervision of employees.   2. Office management.   I. Topchik, Gary S.   II. Title.

HF5549 .12 .B453   2005
658.3'02—dc22

                                                                2004019486

Printing number

10   9   8   7

Contents

Preface

It has truly been an honor to be asked by AMACOM Books to prepare the fifth edition of this book. The first four editions, magnificently written by Loren B. Belker, have been very successful in helping new managers to develop into highly effective leaders within their organizations.

I regret having to say that Loren has passed away. He will be greatly missed by all of those close to him—family, friends, and colleagues—and the countless managers who have been helped by his writing and lectures.

It is with great pride that I have prepared this new edition of *The First-Time Manager*. Loren's insights and deep understanding of the management function go unparalleled. I have just tried to update some of the materials and share my own thoughts on what a successful manager needs to do.

Respectfully,
Gary S. Topchik

Acknowledgments

People often have a greater impact on our lives than they're aware of at the time.

Many people have participated in my management seminars. Their desire to improve their management skills has been their first step in becoming humane and enlightened leaders of people. They've been willing to set aside previously held attitudes of what a manager ought to be.

There are also the organizations and the enterprises that have seen the great value in educating and developing their managers. They have realized that their success directly correlates to the skills and talents of their management teams.

I would like to extend my sincere thanks to my editor and friend, Adrienne Hickey, editorial director at AMACOM. Her insights and encouragement on the revisions and new editions have played a major role in the success of this book.

Finally, I would like to acknowledge my life partner, friends, especially Alexandra, and family members. They have been my source of encouragement and inspiration.

—GST

Introduction

So, what exactly is a new manager supposed to do? You have no doubt met bosses who feel that their job is to tell others what to do. Unfortunately, these managers really have not learned what their role is. It is not to direct people, although some of that may be needed. Rather, management should be the process of getting people to become self-directed. The fifth edition of *The First-Time Manager* will enable you to do that.

Application of the principles described in this book should benefit anyone who is about to embark on a managerial career. Our relationship with other human beings is the most challenging opportunity that exists for us. It covers all aspects of our lives.

If you are going to be a respected manager, you need to find opportunities to gain the support and commitment of your direct reports without having to use your positional power (your title) over them. The best managers get their team members to willingly do what they are supposed to, as opposed to doing it only because the manager said so.

There are many books published on the subject of management, but few of these books address—or zero in on—those individuals who are about to begin a career of leading other people. These first-time managers are not interested in a lot of academic jargon; rather, they are in a state of mixed emotion—absolutely delighted with the promotion and absolutely panic-stricken with the realization that from now on they'll be judged by how well their direct reports perform.

This book is for those people, not for top management with twenty years' experience, even though many top managers would do well to refresh their acquaintance with some of the basic principles that will be discussed in this book. In fact, a comment often heard at seminars for new managers is, "My boss needs this information and these skills even more than I do." This then, creates for the new manager the problem of how you manage in an environment where your own manager violates principles and concepts that you practice and believe in. This new edition helps you succeed with your direct reports, even though your managers and your organization may not be doing exactly what they should be.

This book is written in a conversational manner, making it easy for you to follow along and absorb the ideas presented. You'll find it easy to refer back to specific areas when problems arise in the future. After several months of managing people, reread the book. Many of the concepts will take on additional usefulness at that time.

New chapters have been added in this fifth edition, and many others have been modified or enlarged. For example, there is expanded information on building trust and confidence, performance appraisals, motivating other people, being an active listener, dealing with resistance to change, managing a diverse group of individuals, and building a team environment.

Lastly, almost all the problems you will encounter as a new manager may be new to you, but they've been experienced by many others. The challenges you encounter are balanced by the joy and satisfaction of a management job well done.

Thanks for deciding to spend some time with *The First-Time Manager*.

PART ONE

SO YOU'RE GOING TO
MANAGE PEOPLE

1

The Road to Management

There are many different ways that individuals become managers.

Unfortunately, many companies don't go through a very thorough process in choosing those who are to be moved into managerial positions. Often the judgment is based solely on how well the person is performing in the currently assigned task. The best performer doesn't always make the best manager, although many companies still make the choice on that basis. The theory is that successful past performance is the best indicator of future success. However, management skills are very different from the skills one needs to succeed as an individual contributor.

So, the fact that an employee is a good performer, even though it demonstrates a success pattern, doesn't necessarily mean the person will be a successful manager. Being a manager requires skills beyond those of being an excellent technician. Managers need to focus on people, not just tasks. They need to rely on others, not just be self-reliant. Managers are also team oriented and big picture oriented, whereas nonmanagers succeed by being individually oriented and detail oriented.

Management Is Not for Everyone

Some companies have management-training programs. These programs vary from excellent to horrible. Too often, the program is given to people who already have been in managerial positions for a number of years. Even experienced managers periodically should be given refresher courses in management style and techniques. However, if a training program has any merit, it should be given to individuals who are being considered for management positions. While helping them to avoid mistakes, the training program also gives trainees the opportunity to see whether they will be comfortable leading others.

Unfortunately, far too many organizations still use the "swim or sink" method of management training. All employees who move into supervisory positions must figure it out on their own. This method assumes that everyone intuitively knows how to manage. They don't. Managing people is crucial to the success of any organization; but in too many cases, it is left to chance. Anyone who has worked for any length of time has observed situations where a promotion didn't work out and the person asked for the old job back. There is an old cliché that goes like this: "Be careful what you wish for, because you just might get it." In many companies, the opportunities for promotion are limited if you don't go into management. As a result, some people go into management who shouldn't be there—and they wouldn't want to be in management if other opportunities existed for salary increases and promotion.

A series of management seminars was conducted for one company that used an enlightened approach to the problem of moving the wrong people into management. Everyone under potential consideration for a first-line management position was invited to attend an all-day seminar on what is involved in the management of people. Included were some simple but typical management problems. When these candidates were invited to attend, they were told by the company, "If after attending this seminar you decide that the management of people is not something you want to do, just say so. That decision will in no way affect other nonmanagement promotion possibilities or future salary decisions in your current position."

Approximately 500 people attended these seminars, and approximately 20 percent decided they did not want to move into management. After getting a brief taste of management, approximately 100 people knew they would not make good managers, but they were still valuable employees. Far too many people accept management promotions because they feel (often rightly so) that they will be dead-ended if they reject the promotion.

The Omnipotent

There are some people who believe that if you want something done right, you'd better do it yourself. People with this attitude rarely make good leaders or managers because they have difficulty delegating responsibility. Everyone has seen these people: They delegate only those trivial tasks that anyone could perform, and anything meaningful they keep for themselves. As a result, they work evenings and weekends and take a briefcase home as well. There is nothing wrong with working overtime. Most people occasionally must devote some extra time to the job, but those who follow this pattern as a way of life are poor managers. They have so little faith in their direct reports that they trust them with nothing important. What they are really saying is that they don't know how to properly train their people.

There is usually a staff turnover problem in a section with this kind of manager. The employees are usually more qualified than the "omnipotent" believes and they soon tire of handling only trivia.

You probably know of an omnipotent in your own office or plant. It is a problem if you're working for one, because you'll have a difficult time being promoted. Caught up in your impossible situation, you're not given anything responsible to do. As a result, you never get a chance to demonstrate what you can do. Omnipotents seldom give out recommendations for promotion. They are convinced that the reason they must do all the work is that their staff doesn't accept responsibility. They can never admit that it is because they refuse to delegate. Particular attention has been given to omnipotents, primarily so that you don't allow yourself to fall into this mode of behavior.

One other unvarying trait of omnipotents is that they seldom take their vacations all at once. They only take a couple days off at a time because they are certain the company can't function longer than that without them. Before going on vacation, they will leave specific instructions as to what work is to be saved until their return. In some situations, they'll leave a phone number where they can be reached in an emergency. Of course, they define what the emergency might be. The omnipotent even complains to family and friends, "I can't even get away from the problems at work for a few days without being bothered." What omnipotents don't say is that this is exactly the way they want it because it makes them feel important. For some omnipotent managers, their retirement years are demolished because retirement means abolition of their reason for living, their dedication to the job, and their perceived indispensability.

The Chosen Few

Sometimes, people are also chosen to head a function because they're related to or have an "in" with the boss. Consider yourself fortunate if you do not work for this type of company. Even if you *are* related to the boss, it's very difficult to assume additional responsibility under these circumstances. You doubtless have the authority, but today's businesses aren't dictatorships and people won't perform well for you just because you've been anointed by upper management. So, if you're the boss's son or daughter or friend, you really need to prove yourself. You'll get surface respect or positional respect, but let's face it—it's what people really think of you, not what they say to you, that matters and that affects how they perform.

In the best organizations, you're not chosen for a managerial position because of your technical knowledge. You're chosen because someone has seen the spark of leadership in you. That is the spark you must start developing. Leadership is difficult to define. A leader is a person others look to for direction, a person whose judgment is respected because it is usually sound. As you exercise your judgment and develop the capacity to make sound decisions, it becomes a self-perpetuating characteristic. Your faith in your own decision-making power is fortified. That feeds your self-confidence, and with more self-confidence, you be-come less reluctant to make difficult decisions.

Leaders are people who can see into the future and visual-ize the results of their decision making. Leaders can also set aside matters of personality and make decisions based on fact. This doesn't mean you ignore the human element—you never ignore it—but you deal always with the facts themselves, not with people's emotional perception of those facts.

People are chosen to be managers for a variety of reasons. If you're chosen for sound reasons, your acceptance by your new direct reports will, for the most part, be much easier to gain.

2

Starting Out

Your first week on the job as a manager will be unusual, to say the least. If you're a student of human behavior, you'll observe some surprising developments.

Settling In

Don't believe that everyone is happy about the choice of the new kid on the block. Some of your coworkers will feel *they* should have been chosen. They may be jealous of your new promotion and secretly hope you fall on your face.

Others, the office "yes people," will immediately start playing up to you. As the chosen one, you can be their ticket to success. Their objective isn't all bad, but their method of operation leaves something to be desired.

Some coworkers will put you to the test early. They may ask you questions to see if you know the answers. If you don't, they'll want to see if you'll admit it or if you'll try to bluff your way through it. Some may ask you questions you cannot possibly know the answers to yet, for the sheer delight of embarrassing you.

Most—you hope the majority—will adopt a wait-and-see

attitude. They're not going to condemn or praise you until they see how you perform. This attitude is healthy and all you really have a right to expect.

You will be measured initially against your predecessor in the position. If that person's performance was miserable, yours will look great by comparison even if it's mediocre. If you follow a highly capable performer, your adjustment will be tougher. Before you begin thinking it's best to follow a miserable performer, consider the load of tough problems you would be inheriting from your inept predecessor, which is why you're there. The highly capable predecessor is probably gone because he or she was promoted. So, in either case, you have a big job ahead of you.

One of your first decisions should be to refrain from immediately instituting changes in the method of operation. (In abnormal situations, top management may have instructed you to go in and make certain immediate changes because of the seriousness of the situation. In such cases, however, it is usually announced that changes will be forthcoming.) Above all, be patient. If you make changes immediately, you'll be resented. Your actions will be construed as being arrogant and an insult to your predecessor. Many young new leaders make their own lives more difficult by assuming they have to use all their newfound power immediately. The key word should be *restraint*. Whether or not you want to admit it, you're the one who is on trial with your subordinates, not they with you.

This is a good time to make an important point about your own attitude. Many new managers communicate rather well upward to their superiors, but poorly downward to their direct reports. Your direct reports will have more to say about your future than your superiors. You are going to be judged by how well your section or department functions, so the people who now work for you are the most important in your business life. Believe it or not, they're more important even than the president of your company. This bit of knowledge has always seemed obvious, yet many new managers spend almost all their time planning their upward communication and give only a passing glance to the people who really control their future.

Using Your New Authority

If there is one area that many new managers blunder into, it is
the use of authority. This is particularly true of new managers
who are navigating their way through a self-directed "swim or
sink" method of on-the-job training. It is the idea that because
you now have the authority of management, you must start
using it—and you must use and display it in a big way. It may
be the biggest mistake that new managers make.

View the authority of the new position as you would a
storehouse of supplies. The fewer times you take supplies from
the storehouse, the greater is the supply that remains there for
when it is *really* needed.

The newly appointed manager who starts acting like "the
boss" and begins issuing orders and other directives is off to a
bad start. While you may not hear the remarks directly, the typical comments made behind the back of such a misguided manager might be, "Boy, is she drunk with power," or "This job has
really gone to his head," or "His hat size has gone up two sizes
since he was promoted." You don't need this kind of problem.

If you don't go to the storehouse of authority too often, the
authority you may have to use in an emergency is more effective
because it is infrequently displayed. The people you supervise
know that you are the manager. They know that the request you
make carries the authority of the position. The vast majority of
the time, it is unnecessary to use that authority.

There is a term in the creative arts called *understatement*. For
the most part, it means that what is left unsaid may be as important as what is said. This is true with the use of authority. A
direction given as a request is a managerial type of understatement. If the response is not forthcoming, you can always clarify
or add a bit of authority. On the other hand, if you use all your
authority to achieve a task, and then discover by the reaction
that you have used too much, the damage is done. It is difficult,
if not impossible, to de-escalate the overuse of that authority.

In short, do not assume that you need to use the authority
of your position. Perhaps the greatest by-product of this softer
approach is you are not building a negative image that may be
nearly impossible to erase later.

Having the Personal Touch

Sometime during the first sixty days on the job, you should plan on having a personal conversation with each of the people in your area of responsibility. Don't do this the first week or so. Give your reports a chance to get used to the idea that you are there. When it comes time to talk, the conversation should be formal in nature. Ask your reports into your office for an unhurried discussion about anything that is on their minds. Do no more talking yourself than necessary. This first formal discussion is not designed for you to communicate with the others; it is designed to open lines of communication from them to you. (Have you ever noticed that the more you allow the other person to talk, the higher you'll be rated as a brilliant conversationalist?)

Although the employee's personal concerns are important, it is preferable to restrict the discussion to work-related topics. Sometimes it is difficult to define these limits because problems at home may be troubling the employee more than anything else, but at all times you must avoid getting into a situation where you're giving personal advice. Just because you've been anointed as the boss, it doesn't make you an expert on all the personal problems confronting your people. Listen to them; often that is what they need more than anything else—someone to listen to them.

Getting to Know Them

Now let's get back to your conversation with your team members. The purpose is to give them the opportunity to open the lines of communication with you. Show a genuine interest in their concerns; learn what their ambitions are within the company. Ask questions that will get them to expand on their points of view. You can't fake genuine interest in others; you're doing this because you care about the employees' well-being. Such attention is advantageous to both sides. If you can help employees achieve their goals, they'll be more productive. What is more important is their belief that they're making progress toward their goals.

So your goal in these early conversations is to let your team members know you care about them as individuals and you're there to help them achieve their goals. Let them know you want to help them solve whatever problems they may be having with the job. Establish a comfort zone in which they can deal with you. Make them feel that it is perfectly natural for them to discuss small problems with you. By discussing small problems and small irritants, you can probably avoid most of the larger problems.

You'll discover in your first few months as a manager that your technical abilities are not nearly as important as your human abilities. The majority of your problems are going to revolve around the human and not the technical aspects of the job. Unless your responsibilities are technically complex, you'll discover that if you have outstanding human skills, you can overlook your minor technical deficiencies. Conversely, even if you are the most technically competent manager in the office, without human skills you'll have great difficulty.

Having Friends in the Department

One of the problems many new executives confront is handling friendships with people in the department who now become their employees. This is a difficult situation to which there is no perfect answer. One of the most common questions new managers ask is, "Can I still be friends with the people who used to be my coworkers and who are now my employees?

It is obvious that you shouldn't have to give up your friendships simply because you've received a promotion. However, you don't want your friendships to hurt your performance or the performance of your friends.

It is a mistake to allow your friendships to interfere with your method of operation. A direct report who is truly a friend will understand the dilemma in which you find yourself.

You must be certain that coworkers who were your friends before you became their supervisor receive the same treatment as everyone else. And that doesn't just mean favoring them over other workers. They must not be treated worse merely to prove to the others how unbiased you are.

Although it is certainly true that you can be friends with people, you cannot expect to be friends with them in the same way in the context of work. As a new manager, you will need to establish some expectations of how you will work with all of your team members, whether they are friends or not. You need to hold all individuals to the same rules, regulations, and accountability standards. Also keep in mind that what might look like friendship to you can often look like favoritism to others.

There is a temptation to use your old friend in the department as a confidant. You do not want to give the impression that you are playing favorites. In fact, you must not play favorites. If you do need a confidant, it is preferable to use a manager in another department or section of the organization.

Managing Your Mood

People who report to you are very aware of what kind of mood you are in, especially if you tend to have wild mood swings. Temper tantrums have no place in the work habits of a mature manager—and maturity has nothing to do with age. Letting your irritation show occasionally can be effective, as long as it is sincere and not manipulative.

All of us, from time to time at the office, fall under the spell of moods that reflect outside situations that are troubling us. Many books on management tell us we must leave our problems at the door, or at home, and not bring them into the office. That attitude is naive, because few people can completely shut off a personal problem and keep it from affecting how they perform on the job.

There is little doubt, however, that you can minimize the impact a problem has on your work. The first step is to admit that something is irritating you and that it may affect your relationship with your coworkers. If you can do that, you can probably avoid making other people victims of your personal problem. If an outside problem is gnawing at you and you need to deal with an employee in a critical situation, there is nothing wrong with saying to the employee, "Look, I'm really not in the greatest mood today. If I seem a little irritated, I hope you'll forgive me." This kind of candor is refreshing to a subordinate.

Never think for a moment that others don't have the ability to judge your moods. By showing dramatic changes of mood, you become less effective. In addition, your direct reports will know when to expect these changes, what the telltale signs are, and they will avoid dealing with you when you're on the bottom swing of such a mood. They'll wait until you're on the high end of the pendulum.

Managing Your Feelings

You should work hard at being even-tempered. But it is not a good idea to be the kind of manager who is never bothered by anything—a person who never seems to feel great joy, great sorrow, or great anything. People will not identify with you if they believe you disguise all your feelings.

Keeping your cool all the time is another matter. There are good reasons for keeping your cool. If you can always remain calm, even in troubled situations, you're more likely to think clearly and so be in a better position to handle tough problems. It's also important that you show feelings once in a while, however, or people will think you're a management robot.

To be an outstanding manager of people, you must care about people. That doesn't mean taking a missionary or social worker approach toward them, but if you enjoy their company and respect their feelings, you'll be much more effective in your job than the supervisor who is mostly "thing" oriented.

This, indeed, is one of the problems companies bring on themselves when they assume that the most efficient worker in an area is the one who should be promoted to management. That worker may be efficient because of being thing oriented. Moving these so-called experts into areas where they supervise others doesn't automatically make them "people" oriented.

3

Building Trust and Confidence

Building confidence is a gradual process. One of your main goals is to develop the trust and confidence of your employees, both in their own abilities and in their opinion of you. They must have confidence that you are competent at your job and that you are fair.

The Success Habit

Building confidence in employees is not an easy task. Do you believe success is habit forming? Confidence is built on success, so give your people horses they can ride. Especially in dealing with new employees, assign them tasks they can master. Build in them the habit of being successful, starting small with small successes.

Occasionally a team member will perform a task incorrectly or just plain blow it. How you handle these situations has a great impact on the confidence of employees. Never correct them in front of others. According to the old credo, "Praise in public, criticize in private." The adage still has a lot of management truth in it.

Even when you talk to a team member in private about an error, your function is to train that person to recognize the nature of the problem so as not to make the same error again. Your attitude about errors will speak louder to an employee than the words you use. Your statements must be directed toward correcting the misunderstanding that led to the error and not toward personal judgment. Never say or do anything that will make the employee feel inadequate. You want to build confidence, not destroy it. If you get pleasure from making team members feel foolish, then you'd better start examining your own motives, because you can't build yourself up by tearing someone else down. Examine the error based on what went wrong, where the misunderstanding occurred, and go on from there. Treat the small error routinely; don't make it bigger than it really is.

Let's briefly discuss the "praise in public" part of the old credo. This concept used to be taken as gospel until managers found that it too could also create problems. The individual on the receiving end of the praise felt warm and fuzzy about the compliment, but others who were not equally commended reacted negatively. The disappointment was then directed at the employee who was praised. That is why it is important to be cautious about praising in public. Why make life tougher for that employee by creating jealousy or resentment in the people he or she must work with eight hours a day? If you really want to praise someone expansively for outstanding performance, do it in the privacy of your office. You'll get the pluses without the negatives of resentment and jealousy from coworkers. On the other hand, if you have a group that works well together, respects the efforts of each member of the team, and they are accomplishing their goals, praising in public will be a morale booster for the entire team.

For now, let's amend the old credo to read: "Praise in public or private (depending on the preference of the individual and the dynamics of your team), criticize in private."

You can also build confidence by involving your people in some of the decision-making processes. Without delegating any of your supervisory responsibilities to them, allow them to have some major input into matters that affect them. A new task about to be performed in your area presents the opportunity to give your subordinates some input. Solicit ideas from them on how the new task might best be worked into the daily routine. Given this kind of participation, the new routine will succeed because it is everyone's routine, not just yours. This doesn't mean your staff is making decisions for you; what I'm suggesting is that by involving your people in the process that leads up to your decision, you'll have them working with you rather than accepting new systems imposed on them.

The Evils of Perfectionism

Some managers expect perfection from their employees. They know they won't get it but they feel they'll get closer to it by demanding it. By insisting on perfection, you may in fact defeat your own purposes. Some employees will become so self-conscious about making a mistake that they slow their performance down to a crawl to make absolutely certain they don't screw up. As a result, production goes way down and employees lose confidence.

Another drawback to being a perfectionist is that everyone resents you for it. Your direct reports believe you are impossible to please and you prove it to them every day. This also shatters employee confidence. You know what the acceptable standards for work performance are in your company—no one can blame you for wanting to be better than the average—but you'll have far more success if you get the employees involved in helping decide how to improve performance. If it is their plan, you have a significantly better chance of achieving your goal.

You can also build confidence by developing esprit de corps within your own area. Make sure, however, that the feeling you build is supportive of the prevailing company spirit and not in competition with it.

The Importance of Building Trust

In addition to allowing mistakes and helping individuals see their errors, giving praise and recognition, involving others in the decision-making process, and avoiding perfectionism, you, the manager, can build trust in many other ways.

- You can share the vision of the organization and the department with your team members. Doing this gives them a clearer picture of what the goals are and how they are helping in meeting them.
- You can give individuals clear directions. That shows them that you know what you are doing and are keeping things on track.
- You can share examples of how you have succeeded and what mistakes you have made. Doing that makes you real to your team.
- You can talk to each of your team members to learn what each one wants from the job. By doing this, you are demonstrating that you really care.

All of these additional strategies can build a trusting environment. Think of some others not mentioned here that you could do in your work environment.

4

Show Your Appreciation

In the last chapter, the importance of giving positive feedback or praise is briefly mentioned. It is the best method for motivating individuals and building a positive work environment. Many managers do not give their direct reports praise, which is a big mistake. Praise lets employees know that you care about what they are doing. It also lets employees know that their work is important. If you think about it, it probably takes only seconds to give someone praise and it does not cost a thing! It does have a big impact on most employees though. You can praise people face-to-face, over the telephone, or via e-mail. Face-to-face is always the best method for giving feedback. But if you have employees in other locations or cannot get to them in a timely manner, use the telephone or send e-mail.

Many managers might not show their appreciation because they never had appreciation shown to them by others. You should stop that cycle. Show appreciation. Some managers feel that employees are supposed to perform well because they are getting paid to do well, so there is no reason to praise them for doing so. This is not good reasoning. Those managers should bear in mind that if they praised their employees, they might perform even better. Considering it costs nothing and is real quick, why not do it?

There are many managers, especially newer ones, who are

uncomfortable giving praise. It is a new skill for them. This is to be expected. In order to become more comfortable expressing appreciation, you have to do it. The more you practice it the easier it will become. Consider some of the following points when giving praise or showing appreciation:

• *Be specific.* If managers want certain behaviors repeated, they need to be specific in the type of positive feedback they give. The more detailed the manager is, the more likely the behavior or action will be repeated.

• *Describe the impact.* Most team members like to know how their work ties into the bigger picture or the larger scheme of things such as meeting the objectives of the unit, department, or organization.

• *Do not overdo it.* Many managers go to extremes when they give positive feedback. They give their team members too much positive feedback. When this occurs, the impact of the important feedback is diminished and the praise may seem insincere.

The Actual Skill

Giving praise or appreciation involves two steps. First, you specifically describe the behavior, action, or performance that deserves the appreciation. For example, "I like the new design for the cover of our products catalog." Then you describe why it deserves your appreciation (the business impact). For example, "The new design is bound to greatly increase sales."

Remember, do not be stingy with your appreciation.

You should even give praise to your managers when (on those rare occasions) they deserve it! After all, they are people too and like most people would appreciate positive feedback.

To underscore this point, at a group of thirty attendees in a management seminar, the following two questions were asked:

1. What is the best example of enlightened management you've ever seen?

2. What is the worst example of management you've experienced?

It was no surprise that nearly all the responses had to do with some form of appreciation either received or denied when the staff member felt it was deserved. What was surprising was the depth of emotion displayed about the subject.

One answer was a classic: A young man recounted how he was asked to get in a pickup truck and drive fifty miles to an outlying facility to make an important repair. At 10:30 P.M., after he had just returned home, the phone rang. It was his manager. "I just called to make sure that you got home okay. It's kind of a bad night out there." The manager did not even ask about how the repair went, which indicated his complete confidence in the young man's ability. The manager inquired only about his safe return. The incident had taken place more than five years earlier, but to the young worker, it was as fresh as though it had happened last night.

In a poll conducted by one of the United States' major companies, employees were asked to rank work attributes they considered important. Salary came in sixth. What came in first, by a wide margin, was "a need to be appreciated for what I do."

If appreciation is important to you in your relationship with your manager, realize that it is equally important to the people you manage. When people deserve appreciation, do not withhold it. It does not cost a single dollar, but it is so much more valuable than money.

5

Being an Active Listener

One of the best-kept secrets of successful management is the ability to listen actively. Active listening means letting the other person know that they have been listened to. You do this by involving yourself in the conversation, making clarifying statements, asking questions, summarizing what you have heard, and using appropriate visual and vocal cues. The best listeners are active ones. New managers should be concerned about their ability to communicate and listen actively. Many new managers have the mistaken idea that the minute they are promoted everyone is going to hang on to every word they say. They set out to fill that need. That is the wrong approach. These managers should remember they have two ears and one mouth; therefore, they ought to do twice as much listening as talking.

Active listening is one of the most valuable traits that a new manager can demonstrate for two important reasons: First, if you do a great deal of active listening, you will not be thought of as a know-it-all, which is how most people perceive someone who talks too much. Second, by doing a lot of active listening and little talking, you'll learn what is going on. You'll learn none of it by doing all the talking.

Most people are not good active listeners, and we ought to examine the reason why not.

The Poor Listener

Many people believe that the most beautiful sound in the world is their own voice. It is music to their ears. They cannot get enough of it, so they require others to listen to it. Typically, these people are more interested in what they are going to say themselves than in what others are saying. Indeed, most people can remember nearly everything they have said and hardly any of what the other person has said. People listen partially. They are not being active listeners. They are too busy thinking of the clever things they are going to utter.

If you don't remember anything else about this chapter, you'll do yourself immeasurable good by recalling this statement: If you want to be thought of as a brilliant manager, be an active listener.

Many managers, both new and not so new, do too much talking and not enough listening. You learn very little while you are talking, but you can learn a great deal while listening. New managers often think now that they are in charge, everyone is hanging on to every word. The more you talk, the more you run the risk of boring others. The more you listen, the more you learn. It seems like an obvious choice, especially for a manager of people.

Another reason people are not good listeners is the comprehension gap. Most people communicate at between 80 and 120 words per minute. Let's assume 100 words per minute as the average speaking speed. People can comprehend at a much higher rate. Those who have taken a rapid reading course, and who maintain the skill, can comprehend well over 1,000 words per minute. If someone is speaking at 100 words per minute to a listener who can comprehend at 1,000 words per minute, there is a 900-word-per-minute comprehension gap. A speaking speed of 100 words per minute doesn't demand our full attention, so we tune out the speaker. We think of other things, and periodically we check back in with the speaker to see if anything interesting is going on. If we become more interested in what we are thinking of than in what the speaker is saying, it may be quite a while before we tune back in to what the person is saying.

Everyone has a need to be listened to. What a wonderful service we provide, therefore, if we are great active listeners. The manager who is a great active listener fills an important need for every employee on the staff.

The Active Listener

Active listeners possess several traits and skills, all of which can be developed over time. For one thing, they encourage the other person to talk. When listeners finally talk, they don't turn the conversation back to themselves. They continue the other person's line of communication. They use certain phrases or gestures to signal to the talker that they are truly interested in what he or she has to say.

Looking at someone who is talking to you indicates that you're interested in what the person has to say—that, in fact, you are hanging on every word. Nodding your head affirmatively occasionally indicates that you understand what the talker is saying. Smiling at the same time indicates that you are enjoying the conversation.

When discussing a problem with an employee, other thoughts are likely to enter your mind. You need to take control of those thoughts. While the person is discussing the problem, try to anticipate where the thought is going. What questions are likely to be asked? If someone is suggesting solutions to a problem, try to think of other solutions. Ideally, you should focus 100 percent on what the person is saying, but the comprehension gap is a reality. By controlling your stray thoughts, you can stay focused on the subject at hand, rather than on some extraneous idea that will be distracting.

A well-placed comment also indicates to the talker that you have a genuine interest in what he or she has to say.

"That's interesting."

"Tell me more."

"Why do you suppose she said that?"

"Why did you feel that way?"

In fact, just saying, "That's interesting. Tell me more," will make you a brilliant conversationalist in the minds of everyone with whom you come in contact.

Being an active listener also means that all three forms of communication are in accord. That means that the words you use, your facial expressions, and your voice tone or expression all give the same meaning. The speaker will receive a confusing message if you say, "That's interesting. Tell me more," but have a frown on your face or are speaking in a sarcastic tone. Another mixed message is to respond well verbally but look away from the speaker or become distracted by a document. Would you have confidence that this listener was really interested in what you were saying?

Conversation Terminators

Once a manager achieves a reputation for being an outstanding listener, the staff lines up to discuss many matters. Some will overstay their welcome. They may even think talking to you beats working. You need to have some tools in your managerial toolbox to wind up these conversations.

The verbal conversational terminators are known to just about anyone who has held a job.

"I appreciate your coming in."

"It was nice talking to you."

"Let me think about that a while and get back to you."

There are also some more subtle conversation terminators that you may have seen. You should be aware of them for two reasons: first, so that you can immediately recognize them when a more experienced executive uses them on you, and second, so you can use them when they seem appropriate.

If you've ever had a conversation in someone's office and, while you're talking, watched your host reach over and rest a hand on the telephone receiver even though the telephone hasn't rung, that's a conversation terminator. It says, "As soon as you leave, I'm going to make a phone call." Another technique is for the person to pick up a piece of paper from the desk and glance at it periodically during your conversation. By holding the paper in his hand, your host is saying, "I have something to take care of as soon as you depart."

Another conversation terminator is the one where the host turns in his chair behind the desk to a side position as though about to get up. If that doesn't work, he stands up. That always gets the message across. This approach may seem too direct, but sometimes it becomes necessary.

Occasionally, you'll have an employee who is having such a good time visiting with you that all the signals are ignored. In that case, a verbal terminator that always works is, "I have really enjoyed the conversation, but I have work to do, and I'm sure you do, too." That is not rude for someone who has ignored all other invitations to depart.

When an employee or colleague comes into your office who you know in advance is not going to pick up any of your signals, you can announce at the beginning that you have only a limited amount of time (which is probably true) and if that is not enough time, then the two of you will need to meet later on. You will find this strategy works quite well. Your visitors will say what they need to within the allotted time frame.

It is important that you recognize these conversation terminators. Of course, you should try to keep your conversations meaningful enough to preclude their use on you and your use of them on others. There are many more, but you'll compile your own list and find that different people have their own favorite conversation terminators.

Listening Summary

People enjoy being around someone who shows a genuine interest in them. Good listening skills carry over into many aspects of both your professional and personal life. The interesting thing is that you can start out using these techniques because you realize people will like being with you. There is nothing wrong with this attitude. You become well liked and your team members get a manager who makes them feel good about themselves.

Everyone gains from such an arrangement. You may need to work hard on your active listening skills, but eventually they'll become second nature. At first, you may consider this type of behavior to be role-playing. But after a while you'll be unable to tell when the role-playing has stopped and it's actually you. What happens is that after practicing these new listening habits, you become very comfortable with them and they become part of your regular behavior. You'll derive a great deal of personal satisfaction from being the kind of person others enjoy being around. You'll also be a much more effective manager.

6

The New Manager's Job and Pitfalls to Avoid

So what is the manager's job really? There are so many ways to answer that question but the most helpful is to look at management much the same as an actor would. As a manager you need to play many roles—coach, setter of standards, performance appraiser, teacher, motivator, and so forth. You select the appropriate role based on the situation you are in and the objectives that you want to accomplish. Often, new managers are given the advice to "just be yourself." This is actually bad advice. It will prevent you from using the different roles that will make you a successful and effective manager.

Another mistake that many new managers make is believing that their role is to be directive; that is, to tell others what to do, how to do it, and make sure it gets done. This may be part of the job or necessary to do sometimes. However, what enables you and your employees to succeed in the long run is getting your employees to become self-directed. This means that you must get their support and commitment, share power with them, and remove as many obstacles to their success as possible.

The Manager's Major Responsibilities

Most management experts would agree that managers have certain main responsibilities no matter where they work or who works for them. These main responsibilities include hiring, communicating, planning, organizing, training, and monitoring. The better and more comfortable you become with these responsibilities the easier the job of managing becomes. These six responsibilities are addressed throughout the book, but let's define them here:

1. *Hiring* is finding individuals with the skills or potential skills and commitment and confidence to succeed on the job.

2. *Communicating* is sharing the vision and goals and objectives of the organizations with your employees. It also means sharing information about what is happening in your department, unit, group, or business community.

3. *Planning* is deciding what work needs to be done to meet the goals of your department that, in turn, meets the goals of the organization.

4. *Organizing* is determining the resources that are needed to perform each job or project and deciding which staff members do what.

5. *Training* is assessing the skill level of each one of your employees to determine their gaps, and then providing opportunities for them to close these gaps.

6. *Monitoring* is making sure that the work is being done and that each of your employees is succeeding on their projects and assignments.

Genuine Concern

One way to perform your job well is to give full attention to the needs of the people in your area of responsibility. Some leaders make the mistake of thinking that the concern they show for their employees will be interpreted as a sign of weakness. Genuine concern, however, is a sign of strength. Showing interest in the welfare of your people doesn't mean you'll "cave in" to unreasonable demands. Unfortunately, many new managers fail to recognize this fact. They are unable to differentiate between concern and weakness.

Your concern must be genuine. You cannot fake it. Genuine concern means seeing that your people are properly challenged, and that they're appropriately rewarded when they perform well.

You can't start off by complacently telling yourself, "I'm going to be Mr. Nice Guy." You must seriously take on the burden of responsibility for these people. In fact, you and your team are mutually responsible to one another. Your team members now look to you for leadership. You must see to it that the objectives of the company and the objectives of your team members are not at cross-purposes. Your people should realize that they can achieve their own objectives only by doing their part in helping the company achieve its overall goals.

The person they look to for leadership is you. You serve as interpreter for the employees. What is the company's policy? You must be certain that you know what it is!

Pitfalls to Avoid

Most first-time managers do not supervise a large group of people. Therefore, there may be a temptation to become overly involved in the work of your six or seven people. As you move up the corporate ladder, you will be responsible for more and more workers. It is impossible to be involved in the detail work of thirty-five people, so begin now to distance yourself from the details of each task and concentrate on the overall project.

One of the dangers for a first-time manager is that you now may be managing someone who does your old job, and you may consider it more important than tasks you did not perform. It is human nature to think that what we do is more important than what others do, but that doesn't work when you're the manager. It is not a balanced approach to management. You must resist the temptation to make your old job your occupational hobby, simply because it is familiar and comfortable.

Often, your first managerial job is a project leader or lead position. You manage others, but you still have tasks of your own to perform; you wear two hats. If this is your situation, you must stay interested and involved in the details for a while. When you move into a full-time management position, however, don't take an occupational hobby with you, lest it distract you from the bigger picture.

Of course, don't carry this advice to the extreme. When some people move into management, they refuse to help their staff at a "crunch and crisis" time. They read management journals while their staff is frantically meeting deadlines; they are now "in management." That is just plain stupid. You can build great rapport with your staff if, at crunch time, you roll up your sleeves and help resolve the crisis.

A Balanced Viewpoint

In all management matters, maintain a sense of balance. You have undoubtedly encountered managers who say, "I'm a big-picture guy; don't bother me with the details." Unfortunately, this trait is true of many managers. They become so big-picture-oriented that they are oblivious to the details that bring the picture together. They also may be insensitive to how much effort is required to complete the detailed work.

Other managers, including many first-time managers who have been promoted from a line position, are so enthralled with detail that the overall objective is lost. It is a case of not being able to see the forest for the trees. Balance is required.

Dealing with
Your Superiors

Chapter 6 discussed a manager's attitude toward his or her employees. It is also important for managers to pay attention to their attitude toward superiors. Their future success depends on both their subordinates and superiors.

If you've just had a big promotion, you're feeling grateful to your boss. You are also pleased that the top executive was perceptive enough to recognize your talent. But your new responsibility demands a new level of loyalty from you. After all, you are now a part of the management team. You can't be a good team member without identifying with the team.

Remember, however, that someone who is your superior in the company isn't necessarily smarter than you. Your boss may be more experienced than you, may have been with the company longer, or may be in the top position for other reasons. It is also possible, however, that your boss performed exceedingly well and is indeed smarter than you.

Loyalty to Them

Loyalty has fallen into widespread disrepute. Blind loyalty has never had much to recommend it, but being loyal doesn't mean selling your soul. Your company and your boss are not out to rip off the world. If they are, they're not worth your loyalty. More important, you shouldn't be working for them.

So let's assume you're convinced that your company's purpose is commendable and you're pleased to be associated with its goals. The kind of loyalty we're talking about has to do with carrying out policies or decisions you morally support. Let's assume your position with the company allows for some input into decisions having to do with your area of responsibility. You must make every effort to see that such input is as thoughtful and as broadly based as possible. Don't be the kind of narrow-sighted manager whose recommendations are designed to benefit only his or her own area of responsibility. When this happens, your advice will no longer be sought because it is not broad-based.

If you make recommendations that are broadly based and represent the greater good of the company, your advice will be sought more often. The important thing here is that your involvement in the decision-making process can be beyond your own managerial level.

On occasion, a decision or policy will be made that is directly contrary to the opinions you've expressed; you'll be expected to support that decision or policy, and you may even have to implement it. Ask your boss why the decision was made, if you don't already know. Find out what important considerations went into formulating the policy. Determine what you can about the processes that led to the decision.

The old philosophy of following the leader blindly no longer holds in today's management circles. Nonetheless, many managers and senior executives doubtless wish blind loyalty still existed.

If you are going to do an outstanding job of managing, you have a right to understand the reasons behind major company decisions and company policy. Perhaps your own manager is one who follows higher authority blindly and guards information about top management as if all of it were top secret—and you're the enemy. In that case, you may need to be more political in how you go about getting the answers to your questions.

If it is a policy that affects other departments, you can find out from people at your own organizational level in those departments. If a friend in Department X has a boss who shares information freely with employees, it may be relatively simple to find out what you want to know over a cup of coffee with your friend.

You Have a Responsibility

When working and communicating with your manager, you have many responsibilities in building a good relationship with this person. You need to do the following:

- Keep your manager informed of your plans, actions, and projects.
- Be considerate of your manager's time and try to schedule appointments or meetings at your manager's convenience.
- Present your arguments and concerns logically and objectively and have examples and facts to back up what you are saying.
- Be willing to listen to your manager's point of view. Your manager might be right!

Dealing with an Unreasonable Manager

We do not live in a perfect world. As a result, at some time in your career, you may be in the uncomfortable position of reporting to a difficult manager—someone who is not doing a good job of managing and/or may be unpleasant to be around. Unfortunately, you cannot fire an incompetent or unreasonable boss, as pleasant as that prospect might be.

Let's be candid. If a long-term manager is difficult, you have to wonder why the situation is allowed to exist. If everyone in the organization knows this person is miserable to work for, why does top management allow the situation to continue?

On the other hand, if everyone else in the department thinks the manager is doing a great job and you're the only one having a problem, it's a far different situation. If you are new to the department, you might give it some time by not reacting too quickly. The problem may resolve itself if you do a great job and are not hypersensitive. You may find it is style and not substance.

If your manager is really causing problems for you or your direct reports, however, you definitely need to do something about it. You do have some viable choices. Depending on the political environment and culture of your organization, different strategies may work better. Right off the bat, you should try to communicate directly with your boss. Tell him or her what is up. Explain in a professional manner how your manager's behaviors, policies, or actions are having a bottom line business impact. For example, suppose your manager is giving different instructions to the staff than you are. This is causing shipping delays and customer complaints—bottom-line concerns. Even if he or she doesn't like hearing it, your boss should appreciate your directness in pointing out this problem.

Often bosses do not realize that they may be doing something inappropriate. They need the feedback. You should always try to meet with your boss on a regular basis to discuss any issues that need addressing. If your manager doesn't think these meetings are necessary, you should insist. Try to explain how constant communication will prevent problems from springing up and how you would both benefit from this undertaking.

On another note, I always advise new managers that if a mentor is not assigned to them, they should find one on their own. You need someone within the organization who is well respected and aware of the political goings-on. You need someone who can take you under his or her wing and teach you about organizational life.

Now, let's say you have the type of boss who does not like to get feedback from employees. So what do you do now? Here is where understanding the politics and culture of your organization comes in and where your mentor can be of great assistance. You may need to get someone else to speak to your boss. It could be someone on his or her level, a mutual friend who you have in the organization, human resources—if their reputation is good and they play fair—or you may have to take the biggest risk of all and jump levels to have that person's boss speak to him or her. Keep in mind that when you do this, you probably will sever your relationship with your boss forever. But you may have no other choice. You are undertaking this action for your team or the overall benefit to the organization.

You do have one final option. You may have to say to yourself: "The boss is difficult. She has been difficult for many years; no one seems to care or is willing to change her behavior. This may not be the best place for me since my boss has a great influence on my success. Perhaps I need to find a position in another department or within another organization."

Driving Good People Away

It is true that there are many companies that take advantage of a downturn in the economy to drive their people harder, recognizing that it's more difficult for people to leave. There are reasons why such an attitude is shortsighted. First, top-flight people can always find other jobs, no matter how tough the economy. The lesser talented people are the ones who cannot. So, this maladjusted company attitude drives away the more talented and retains the less talented. That is a recipe for mediocrity. Second, in a tough economy, appreciating all of your staff, including the very talented managers, places the organization in a stronger position to compete effectively. A company with a talented and appreciated staff will beat the brains out of a company that treats its employees merely as units of production. The long-range prospects for the latter style are not good.

One of the surest ways to eventually drive good people from your company is to perpetuate bad management. This may sound obvious, but many new managers can't wait to start treating their people the way they've been treated. They may be taught the more humane management approach, but they go with what they know. They are anxious to take their turn "dishing it out" after all these years of "taking it."

The lesson of the unreasonable boss is to be the kind of leader you wish you had, not to carry on the tradition. Do not adopt a management style you hate and get even with people who had nothing to do with your mistreatment. If you're working for an unreasonable boss, do humanity a favor and say, "Let it end with me."

Knowing Your Manager's Personality Style

There have been countless books and articles written on the topic of managing your boss. The main premise of all these writings is the same: If you know the personality style of your manager, you will be able to manage this person by knowing what your manager needs and wants and how your manager likes to work and communicate. If you can manage this person, you will have fewer problems with him or her.

There are four basic personality types that managers have. Some managers have a distinct personality style while others are combinations of two or three styles. Read the descriptions that follow and see if you can figure out your manager's style. If you can, you will be more successful working with your manager.

The Monopolizers

They like to be in charge of everything. These managers are fast decision makers who stick to their decisions, are very organized, and are bottom-line oriented. They are "my way or the highway" types. If they were doing target practice, their saying would be "ready, fire, aim" (as opposed to the usual saying of "ready, aim, fire"). If you work for monopolizers, make sure you are clear and direct with your communication, have all your facts ready, and be prepared to do what they say.

The Methodicals

They are your analytic types. These managers like to take their time gathering information and data before making a decision. They are very steady and predictable and overly concerned with accuracy. If they were doing target practice, their saying would be "aim, aim, aim." They hate to make decisions and are always looking for more or different information. If you work for methodicals, be patient! Realize that they are trying to make the best decision based on all data. When you give your opinion or your suggestion, make sure that you have analyzed it carefully and can explain your reasoning and logic to them.

The Motivators

These are the superiors who are fun to be around. They are charismatic and seem to have good relationships with everyone in the organization. They have high energy, are creative, and have a competitive spirit. However, they often talk more than they do. They like to get things started, but completing them is another story. If they were doing target practice, their saying would be "talk, talk, talk." They just love to talk and have fun and sometimes the work gets the backseat. When communicating with Motivators, make sure to do a lot of chitchatting. Ask them how their weekend was, how the kids are, and so forth. Before they can get down to business, they need to socialize.

The Mixers

You probably have a relaxed and laid-back work environment if your superior is a Mixer. Mixers have a strong sense of dedication, are loyal team members, patient, sympathetic, understanding, dependable, and great at keeping the peace. Their Achilles heel is that they shy away from conflict. They do not like change. They favor the status quo. They may also be more concerned with how people are doing than getting the work out. If they were doing target practice, their saying would be "ready, ready, ready." They are always there for you. The needs of others come before their own. When working with Mixers, put on your feelings and teamwork hat. You will need it!

8

Choosing a Managerial Style of Your Own

If you look at the history of management style in the United States, you'll notice that two styles have dominated. Managers were either autocratic or diplomatic. Today, however, the best managers know that there are more than two styles of managing and they need to be good in all the styles. Before discussing the necessity of having an alert managerial style, let's look at the autocratic and diplomatic styles.

The Autocrat vs. the Diplomat

It is difficult to believe that we still see the old-fashioned autocrat in management today. You have to wonder why this is so. Partly it has to do with the fact that so many managers are given no training. They are left to find their own way, so they begin acting as they think they should. They think in terms of being a "boss." Autocrats also believe that if they take the softer approach, employees will take advantage. It is as though the softer approach will be seen as a sign of weakness.

Another possibility is that it takes more time to be a diplomatic manager. These managers spend time with people explaining not only *what* is to be done but also *why* it's done. The boss type doesn't want to be bothered. This person's attitude is "Do it because I said so." The diplomat realizes that the more people understand of what and why, the better they perform.

The autocrat wants to make every decision and views the staff as making robotic responses to his or her commands. The autocrat pushes the buttons, the staff snaps to, and it happens. The diplomat knows that the time spent up front, getting everybody involved, pays off with huge dividends down the road.

The autocrat engenders fear while the diplomat builds respect and even affection. The autocrat causes people to mutter under their breath, "Someday, I'll get even with this SOB." The diplomat causes people to say, "He respects us and cares for us. I'd walk the last mile for him. All he needs to do is ask."

The autocrat believes the diplomat is a wimp. The diplomat believes the autocrat is a dictator. The difference is that the autocrat uses authority constantly, while the diplomat is judicious in its display.

People working for the autocrat believe they are working *for* someone. Those reporting to the diplomat believe they are working *with* someone.

The Need for Alertness

As a new manager, you should use the "alertness approach" when selecting an appropriate managerial style. In order to be *alert*, you must use the right amount of *control* and *encouragement* for each of your employees. Control is telling employees what to do, showing them how to do it, and making sure that the work is done. Encouragement is motivating, listening to, and running interference so employees can do what they are expected to do.

Some employees need high amounts of control and encouragement. Others need little control or encouragement. Then there are others who fall somewhere in between. In order to use the alertness approach in selecting a managerial style, you have to determine what each of your employees needs from you. That is, how much control and/or encouragement do they need from you?

The amount of control or encouragement each employee requires will depend on what he or she is working on or what is occurring in the department. For example, if an employee needs to learn how to operate a new piece of equipment, he or she will need a lot of control. If there are talks of downsizing and cutting back throughout the company, your team members will need much encouragement.

The following descriptions will help you see the connection between what your staff needs from you and how much control and/or encouragement you give them; in other words, are you being alert to their needs?

• *Type A.* This is someone who is very motivated to do well but lacks the skill or knowledge to succeed. Being alert, you know this person needs mostly control from you.

• *Type B.* This is someone who has lost his or her motivation but has the skills to do the job. Being alert, you know this person needs lots of encouragement.

• *Type C.* This is someone who performs very well and is also motivated. Being alert, you know this person needs little control and encouragement.

• *Type D.* This is someone who lacks both ability and willingness to perform. Being alert, you know this person—besides a good kick (which, of course you cannot do)—needs lots of control and encouragement.

• *Type E.* This is someone who has medium amounts of skill and motivation. Being alert, you know this person obviously needs medium amounts of control and encouragement.

Let's look at a workplace scenario and see how alert you can be. Suppose you are heading a large independent project at a telecommunications company. One of the employees assigned to you, Andy, is used to working independently on his assignments. Andy likes calling all the shots and really enjoys his work. He always gets excellent results and his internal clients are thrilled with his work. Working on your project, you notice that he finds it challenging to plan and communicate and make decisions with the other team members. In addition, Andy has put down the whole team concept and says it is a waste of time. He has expressed his unhappiness with being on this new project.

Being alert, what type (A to E) is Andy and what does he need from you as his manager? The answer: Even though Andy is an experienced employee in his regular work, this is not true on your project. Andy needs control and encouragement. He needs guidance in how to work with others in a team environment and support for this difficult transition he is making. Andy's type is D for this project, although he is probably an A type on his own assignments.

Here is a suggestion that will make managing much easier for you. Call it "drive time." On the way to work, think about all your direct reports every few days. Think about what their type is on all the different assignments and projects that you have them doing. Then be alert. Think about what they need from you. If you are already giving it to them, you have the perfect scenario. If you are not, decide what you need to do differently. You'll find this one suggestion will make a huge difference for you as a manager. Try it.

9

Building Team Spirit

In recent years, getting work done through teams has become standard practice in many organizations. This is true for a couple of reasons. One reason is synergy. Generally, it has been proved in workplaces that groups make better decisions than any individual working has alone. Another reason for having teams is that in today's world of high technology the manager can not know as much as all of the employees. The manager can no longer be the expert. In many fields and occupations today, managers have people working for them who know more than they do. It is no longer possible in these instances to tell people what to do. The manager needs to support and guide employees and let them come up with the work-related answers.

If you really want your team to succeed and perform at the highest levels possible, you need to build team spirit. Team spirit is the willingness and the ability to work in an interdependent fashion where any team member needs to rely on other team members to accomplish his or her work or to achieve the goals of the team. In order to build a team spirit, the following five factors are essential:

1. Open communication
2. Empowerment
3. Clear roles and responsibilities

4. An effective leader
5. A reward and accountability system for both individual team members and the entire team

Open Communication

Consider this scenario: A young manager-to-be accompanied his mentor, an experienced manager, to observe a high-performing team in operation at a manufacturing company. When he first walked into the room, he said to his mentor, "Oh boy, this is a dysfunctional team! Listen to the way they are arguing with each other." The older man replied, "Pay attention, you are witnessing a great team."

It took the younger man several minutes to understand what the manager meant. This team was in conflict. They were strongly disagreeing with one another as to the best way to improve their product. It is fantastic when a team does this. What more can you ask for than when a team cares so much about the service they are providing or the product that they are producing? They had open, honest communication. What team spirit!

Empowerment

You get a high-spirited team when you give them empowerment—the right to make decisions that concern the work they are doing. Of course, you set boundaries of time, money, choices, and so forth. But once you give the team the final power of decision making, you will notice a confidence, camaraderie, and a feeling of strength emerge. Whatever you do, make sure you do not empower teams that are not ready for it. That is disaster. Many new managers make this big mistake. They probably do it because they want to get into the good graces of the team. Make sure the team is ready for empowerment or you and the organization will suffer from the consequences of their poor decisions.

Clear Roles and Responsibilities

Can you walk up to any one of your team members and have this person clearly define his or her role and responsibilities on the team? Can you walk up to any one of your team members and have this person clearly define the roles and responsibilities of every other team member, including yours as the leader? When team members can do this, they know what is expected of them and what is expected of every other team member. They also know on whom they can count for helping them with their work. All of this leads to a high-spirited team environment.

Effective Leadership

Read the following list. Check off the items that you currently do. Develop an action plan for any items not checked. When you are able to check off all the items, you are doing your part in building a high-spirited team. As leader, you should do the following:

- Set clear goals for each team member and the team.
- Give clear directions for those who need it.
- Share examples and experiences of your personal successes and mistakes in order to relate to the team.
- Emphasize the positive rather than the negative in your talks with your team.
- Give continual feedback to each team member and to the team—both positive and constructive.
- Use small successes to build team cohesiveness.
- Practice what you say.
- Express your and the organization's appreciation through rewards, if available.
- Develop a constructive relationship—both you and the team are working together toward the same goals.
- Make change happen for the better by encouraging creativity and innovation.

- Encourage self-reliance and self-development.
- Encourage team members to express their views during conflict and share yours with them.
- Have your team see its connection to the larger organization and to customers and/or the community.

Reward and Accountability System

This last factor for building a high-spirited team is the responsibility of the organization and the managers working together. Many organizations preach teamwork. You walk around the building and see posters hanging up with happy groups of people working and playing together. You read company mission statements and they say something about being the best team. And people are assigned to teams. But yet teamwork is lacking. Why is this? It is because the organization and its managers do not hold people accountable for working in teams or reward them for it.

If we truly expect people to cooperate with each other for the common good of the organization, we cannot only evaluate them, rate them, or give them performance appraisals just for their individual contribution. We have to do all of that for their team contribution as well. When team members get the message that you are holding them accountable based on how good they are as team players, they quickly get the message that teams count. It beats those posters! You have to do the same thing with the reward system. That is, reward people for both their individual and team contributions.

Some managers claim that it is not a good practice to reward some team members more than others. They say that you will never have high-performing teams if you do that. Those managers should take a look at the most successful professional sports teams. They all have some team members who earn more based on the roles they play or their achievements. It works there and there is great team spirit on those teams. Look at many successful and spirited work teams. You will often find individual team members making higher salaries or getting special rewards for their individual contributions. It works in those situations, and there is great team spirit on those teams as well.

PART TWO

TACKLING YOUR

NEW DUTIES

10

Managing Problem Employees

Not every employee you manage is going to be successful on the job. Someone who is performing poorly may require additional training, transfer to another area where the employee may shine, or ultimately, outright dismissal. Too often, in large companies, managers unload their problem employees onto another department. This is not being fair to your fellow managers, unless you really believe that the employee will do better in a new department where there is a better match for his or her skills. In some companies, I have even seen managers promote their poor performers, just to get rid of them. When asked by the manager of the other department how the prospective candidate is performing in the current job, these managers are not completely candid in their reply. I think the only correct policy in this situation is to be open and honest. Someday you yourself may be looking at people in other departments as candidates for promotion into your own department, and your best guarantee of not getting someone else's rejects is never to deliver that kind of cheap shot yourself.

You can probably relate to the following story involving a first-time manager. After he had reviewed performance appraisals of people one level below the job he was attempting to fill in his division, he selected three likely candidates. As is customary,

he called the managers of these candidates and got a glowing
report about one in particular, a young man. He promoted him
to his department and he ended up being a complete disaster.
He had to terminate him after a short period of time because he
wasn't doing the job. The first-time manager then confronted the
person who had made the recommendation and asked for an
explanation, never dreaming he had been mousetrapped. The
answer he got was that the employee had not been satisfactory
and the manager was tired of dealing with him. Because the
previous manager was not candid, the first-time manager was
tricked into doing the dirty work. He eventually had to terminate the employee.

Of course, there is a great temptation to pay back such a
manager in kind, but the solution is to make sure no one ever
does that to you in the first place. Retaliation in an intracompany
operation is not beneficial to anyone.

Rehabilitation

There'd be nothing wrong, however, in attempting to rehabili-
tate a nonproductive employee if it were done with the full
knowledge of everyone involved. In the situation just described,
for example, had the fellow manager sat down with the first-
time manager and indicated that the employee was not doing a
good job *but* there were strong reasons for wanting him to have
another chance, the first-time manager might have taken the person. There have been many trials like this one that have been
successful. The job and the employee were not a good fit, but
the employee had talent; the move to another area where that
talent could be better used turned a less-than-satisfactory employee into a productive one.

Generally, however, you'll be much more effective as a
leader if you can solve your own problems in your own department and not unload them onto another department. Companies use many testing devices to put people on jobs that are
natural for them, or at least to place them in working areas of
some personal preference. These devices range from simple five-

minute tests to complex three-hour psychological evaluations. This is something your company either already has or should consider having. To emphasize my point again, you must always be conscious of the advantages of fitting employees to jobs at which they have the best chance of being successful. It is much easier to move people around into jobs that are natural for them than to force them into jobs they perform poorly and then try to "educate" them. It just doesn't work all that often.

Serious Personal Problems

Some subordinates have personal problems that hinder their attendance and their performance on the job. You would be quite naive to believe that alcohol, drugs, or serious family difficulties were not going to affect your management responsibilities.

Just because you're a manager doesn't mean you're equipped to handle every problem that comes your way. Many enlightened companies recognize this fact and have established employee assistance programs. These programs are usually community supported, unless the company is large enough to justify an on-site service. Employee assistance programs have professional resources available, have connections with chemical dependency programs, and know all the services that exist within the community.

It's foolish for you as a manager to believe that you have the capacity and the resources to solve any and all problems. If you try to handle a situation beyond your professional competence, you run the risk of making the situation worse. As a manager, your responsibility is to see that the job is done within the boundaries of sound management principles. The employee's personal problem is interfering with accomplishing that objective. Although rescuing a human being is also a legitimate objective, you are swimming in uncharted waters.

Also, under the eyes of the law in most states, a manager is viewed as someone who is not qualified to give personal advice. The following case occurred several years ago in a computer manufacturing company in Salt Lake City. There was an assembly line worker who was late about half of the time, sometimes by as much as forty to fifty minutes. In addition, her performance was going downhill quickly. After a few weeks of this behavior, her manager spoke to her about it. The employee apologized and said that the day care center where she sent her young son often opened late. She said she could not just leave her son on the doorstep and come to work. She also said she worried about her son all day because she did not know how good the center was and this was affecting her performance.

The manager replied, "Take my advice. Send your child to the day care center where I send my children. It opens one hour earlier. If you do this, and I strongly suggest that you do, you will no longer be late and you will not have to worry about his care." The employee heeded the advice of the manager. Without going into the gory details, something unfortunate happened to the employee's young son at this "new" center. The employee, with the assistance of legal council, sued the company and won.

The court ruled that a manager is not qualified to give personal advice. The manager should have referred the individual to human resources or to a qualified service such as employee assistance. Switching day care centers was up to the employee. Of course, you must listen to your employees and be supportive of what they are going through. Keep in mind that all your team members have challenging lives outside of work and they all have made adjustments to be at work.

You will probably need to have a direct confrontation with the problem employee, but you will have to define your *overall* objective first. Your objective is to straighten out a work problem. You need to insist that troubled employees solve their problems, and you can even direct them to the employee assistance program. You have to make it clear that if they choose not to solve the problem, they may be dismissed from employment. Take care not to do this in a cruel, uncaring way, but be sure to be firm so there is no misunderstanding.

You must be willing to listen, but not to the extent that problem employees spend a great deal of time in your office talking when they should be working. There is a fine line between being a good listener and allowing people to get away from their work for two hours while they drink coffee and pour out all their problems to you.

Sooner or later in your management career, you'll hear of every conceivable problem (along with some inconceivable problems). People are involved in the totality of life; they have problems with spouses, children, parents, lovers, coworkers, themselves, religion, diets, feelings of self-worth, and so on.

A cardinal rule in dealing with human frailties, one that will save you endless aggravation, is *don't pass judgment.* Solve the work problem, and point employees to where they can solve their personal problems. In some cases, you may demand that they solve the problem because of what the failure to find a solution is doing to the work environment.

How to Manage Challenging Behavior Types

As a new manager, you are likely to run into many different types of employees whom you will find challenging. When faced with managing them, you must confront their behaviors. If you let these behaviors slide, you are giving the message that it is OK to keep behaving that way. Also, the rest of your staff will lose trust and confidence in you. They will feel you do not have the ability to handle difficult employees or you don't care.

The best way to confront these challenging behaviors is to tell the employees what behaviors they need to change and why. Then you want to listen to them. They may have good reasons for behaving the way they do. Then you need to get them to agree that they will change and discuss how you will monitor their behavior. Make sure to give positive feedback when they show signs of improvement. Of course, you want to come to this "confrontation" meeting prepared with examples of what you mean in case they doubt what you are saying or are not sure what you mean. Be positive and try to help the person change. It will be much easier for you if they do. Having to put someone on a discipline procedure can be a nightmare for everyone. You may have no other choice, but it should always be your last alternative. We will talk more about discipline in Chapter 14.

Here are a few of the types of employees that most new managers find the most challenging. There are many others. Be on the outlook for them. Use the suggestions discussed here for confronting their unacceptable behavior.

The Attacker

This is the person who always disagrees with what you say or with what other team members say. The Attacker tries to undermine you and block the efforts of the group or department from achieving its goals.

The Comic

This employee thinks his or her main job at work is to entertain others. Laughter in the workplace is great, but when done to excess it distracts from getting the job done.

The Deserter

This individual either mentally or physically leaves the team. The Deserter drops out and stops contributing. This person stops performing at work.

The Limelight Seeker

The employee likes to take credit for the work done by others and goes around bragging about how crucial he or she is to the success of the organization.

The Moonlighter

This employee treats his or her regular job as secondary to some other interest. At one company with about 3,500 employees, a manager had trouble figuring out one of his employees, named Joy. From August to January, Joy was the busiest employee you could imagine. She was always on the telephone or her computer or holding meetings in the conference rooms. But from February through July, Joy sat around with nothing to do. Take a wild guess what Joy was up to. She ran the company's football pool and made it her full-time job!

The Not-My-Jobber

This employee does nothing unless it is in his or her job description. If you asked this person to drop something at HR on the way to lunch, he or she would refuse. After all, where does it say that is one of his or her responsibilities or goals?

The Bleeding Heart

These employees feel they given their lives for the company and have received nothing in return, and want everyone to know it. The bleeding heart usually has no life or no enjoyable life outside of work.

The Complainer

This type likes to moan and complain about everything. It could be the workload, the other employees, the boss, the customer, the drive to work, the day of the week, the time of the day, and so on. Complainers are dangerous because their "fever" easily spreads to others.

There are obviously many other types of challenging employees. As a manager, you need to expect all kinds of difficult behaviors and confront them as soon as possible.

11

Hiring and Interviewing

There are probably as many different hiring practices as there are companies. It would be impossible to cover all the various methods, so let's make a couple of simple assumptions. Let's say the human resources department does the initial screening, but you have the ultimate decision-making authority as to who comes to work in your area of responsibility.

The Use of Tests

With greater federal, state, and sometimes city participation in hiring procedures, your company may not do much testing of prospective employees. There are many legal requirements to follow when testing. But testing is among the best ways to determine if candidates really have the skills they claim they do. There are many companies that pay their job candidates for their interview time because they keep them there an entire day in order to test them.

The quality of prospective employees will vary a great deal. When unemployment rates are high, you'll find greater interest being shown in the job and you'll have a larger number of prospects to choose from. The reverse will be true when unemployment rates are low. There are even situations where available employees are so few that you'd consider hiring just about any-one who appeared at your desk. So, there'll be forces beyond your control. We're concerned here with situations you can control.

The Missing Ingredient

Almost without exception, when managers are asked what is the most important ingredient in hiring a new employee, they come up with experience, qualification, or education. They rarely come up with the missing ingredient: *attitude.*

You can hire an employee with all the experience, education, and qualifications you could hope for, but if the person has a bad attitude, you have just hired a problem employee. On the other hand, you can hire a person with less experience, education, and qualifications, and if that person displays an outstanding attitude, in all likelihood you will have an outstanding employee. Every experienced manager will agree that attitude is the most important element in an employee.

The Screening Process

Most managers do too much talking and too little listening during the interview process.

The interview with the prospect is a two-way sizing up. Naturally, the prospect wants the job, so candidates will give you the answers they believe will maximize their chances. Any applicant who doesn't do this isn't bright enough to be hired.

Don't ask questions that are so difficult the prospect can't possibly answer them. Here are some questions to avoid that managers who pride themselves on being tough interviewers might ask:

"Why do you want to work here?"

"What makes you think you're qualified for this job?"

"Are you interested in this job because of the salary?"

Dumb questions like these will make you a rotten interviewer. You must strive to put the prospect at ease so that you
can carry on a conversation. Your aim is to get to know the prospect better, and that means avoiding a confrontation. Rather,
make statements or ask questions that will relax the applicant.
Hold the tougher questions—but not the previous three questions—for later in the process. Consider the following sample
interview.

Mrs. Valencia's Job Interview

The objective ought to be to find out if the applicant meets the
job qualifications and *has a good attitude*. It makes sense to spend
the early part of the interview engaging the applicant in some
nonthreatening small talk.

Most applicants are nervous. They have a great deal riding
on the results. The goal is to put the person at ease. By not immediately going to the business at hand, you let people know
you're interested in them as a person, apart from the job. It is
important that you develop a comfortable relationship. If this
person is going to work for you, it's the beginning of what could
be years of daily contact. Even when candidates don't get the
job, they will feel more kindly toward you and your company
because you've shown a sincere interest in them.

Note: A company has many "publics": the general public,
the customers, the industry it is part of, government agencies
that it comes in contact with, and your employees and those
who apply to be. In one case, a woman who was a substantial
patron of an upscale department store thought that it would be
fun to have a part-time job there. She resented the treatment she
received when she applied for a job, and vowed never to set foot
in the store again. That cost the store thousands of dollars a year
from her purchases alone, not including the purchases all her
friends would have made had she not shared her negative experience with them.

When the small talk is over, you might consider using this
approach: "Mrs. Valencia, before we start talking specifically
about the position you've applied for, I'd like to tell you a little

about our company. Because, while we're considering you, you're also considering us, so we want to answer any questions you may have about our company."

Then go ahead and tell her something about the company. Tell her what your purpose is, but don't spend too much time on statistics. Talk more about the company's relationship with its employees. Tell her anything in this area that is unique. You want her to get a feel for the company and its people. This additional talk is to give her a feel for the company she wishes to be a part of, and it also gives her more opportunity to relax and feel comfortable.

We now arrive at the critical point in the interview. You want to ask questions that are going to give you some clues about this person's attitude. Most people-oriented managers (and that is most of them) cannot stand a vacuum, so if the applicant doesn't respond promptly, they tend to move in and try to help out. It's an act of kindness, but in this case, it interferes with obtaining the crucial information you need to make a proper selection.

Questions to Ask and What You Can Learn

Some sample questions to ask are:

"What did you like best about your last job?"

"What did you like least about your last job?"

"How did you feel about your last manager?"

These are sample questions. You might devise some of your own that seem more appropriate for you, but until you do, consider using the ones suggested here.

Let's examine each question and what "right" and "wrong" answers can tip you off about employee attitude.

If the answer to question 1 mentions items such as the challenge of the job, the fact that the company promotes from within, that the company encourages and assists with educational opportunities, or that self-starters are appreciated, you have indications of someone who has recognized what is important in a sound working environment.

However, if the person's answer mentions things such as the office being closed every other Friday, which makes for nice long weekends; that the company provides many social activities, including both a bowling and a golf league; and that employees receive a paid vacation the first year with the company, you may have an applicant who is looking for a place to socialize. This person may be a social butterfly, and while there is nothing wrong with enjoying the company of others, that should not be the main reason for seeking the job.

Now let's discuss some potential answers to question 2, about the items liked least on the last job. If the answer involves something such as being required to work overtime occasionally, being asked to come in on a Saturday, or being expected to give up a Saturday to go to a community college for acquiring some skills that will be helpful on the job, even though the company paid the seminar fee, those are wrong answers.

However, if the answer mentions that the company had no formal performance appraisal system, that the granting of raises didn't seem to bear any relationship to quality, or that there wasn't anything the person really disliked, but just feels there might be better opportunities elsewhere, those are thoughtful "burn no bridges" responses. Let's now move to question 3. You'll note that the question is more open-ended. If the applicant really trashes her last supervisor and is generally negative, such as, "I don't think I ought to use the kind of language it takes to describe the SOB," that is a negative answer.

Let's assume that the relationship with the last supervisor was terrible, but she answers, "Well, as with many bosses, we had our differences, but I liked and respected her." That is a diplomatic description of what may have been a bad situation.

Questions from Applicants

You may also say to the applicant, "I've been asking you all these questions. Do you have any questions you'd like to ask of me?" The questions asked by the prospect can also provide clues to attitude.

What if questions from the prospect are along these lines?

"How many holidays do you close for each year?"

"How much vacation do you give the first year?

"How long do you have to be here to get four weeks vacation?"

"What social activities does the company sponsor for the employees?"

"What's the earliest age you can retire? How many years of service do you need?"

Questions along this path indicate someone who has an attitude focused on getting out of work rather than into it. These samples are obvious, and again overdrawn to make the point. Some questions asked by the applicant may be subtler than this, but are still a tip-off of an undesirable attitude.

The following sample questions asked by applicants reflect a decidedly different attitudinal bent:

"Are people promoted based on performance?"

"Can an outstanding performer receive a larger salary increase than an average performer?"

"Does the company have regular training programs for the employees, so they can broaden their work skills?"

The thought may have entered your mind that the applicant is giving you the answers he or she thinks you want to hear. If that is so, it indicates you are not interviewing a dummy. Isn't an employee who can anticipate what the answers ought to be going to be a better staff member than an applicant who hasn't a clue as to how to respond? Job prospects who trash a former company or manager, even if deserved, say more about themselves than about the object of scorn. There is no way such an approach will advance the candidate's prospects for the job, so the insightful person will avoid negative comments about past working relationships.

An important strategy the manager brings to the interview process is silence. When a person does not answer right away, the silence may feel uncomfortable but if you jump in, you are not as likely to get the real answer.

The human resources department probably has oriented you in the types of questions that can and cannot be asked. You need to know the areas that you cannot move into because they are discriminatory or illegal, or both.

One forbidden question that comes to mind is, "Do you have to provide child care for children?" Knowing that is one of the topics you cannot broach, if the applicant asks about work hours, do not consider that a negative question. It may be triggered by a concern about child care.

Another question from an applicant that should not be considered a negative has to do with health insurance. An employee asking about health benefits is showing responsibility. In short, it is the general tenor of questions that indicates an attitude problem. You must use your good judgment about which subjects denote attitude and which indicate responsibility.

As you obtain more experience with the interview process, you will become more skilled at it. In most job interviews, employee attitude is completely ignored. Typically, managers hold applications in their hands and say, "Well, I see you worked for the XYZ Company." Look that application over before you sit down with the applicant. Don't see it for the first time in the presence of the applicant. Then ask the questions that reveal work attitudes.

The Effects of Unemployment Rates

If your town has a high unemployment rate, you'll get better acting performances from prospective employees. (If you desperately needed steady work and a steady paycheck, you'd take almost any kind of job. You'd also be more adroit in selling the interviewer on why you should have the job.)

With high unemployment, you'll also run into overqualified applicants. No doubt, you can empathize with these people in their current dilemma. But you should also realize that once other opportunities open up that make it possible for them to cash in on their full qualifications, you will lose these employees. First, if people are working below their capacity, they are not challenged in the job. Second, they are immediately looking for a better job.

Knowing the unwillingness of most managers to hire over-qualified workers, some desperate applicants will shade their qualifications on the application, so that their greater education or experience is hidden. If you hire overqualified people, be pre-pared to lose them.

The Comfort-Zone Underachiever

A comfort-zone underachiever (CZU) is a person who is highly qualified but doesn't like being challenged. There are many of them around, but very few of them admit it.

One of the main problems for CZUs is convincing you they genuinely want to work at a position that seems far below their capacity. They often get burned, in that they're not hired for jobs they want because they're overqualified. They soon discover that the way to handle this is not to list all their qualifications on the job application. The registered nurse who doesn't want to prac-tice nursing may not indicate her training in that field. She may trim her list of qualifications to fit the clerical job she wants. Likewise, the schoolteacher who really can't stand young chil-dren in a classroom environment may not list all his credentials. Handling previous work experience on the job application gets more difficult because the trained interviewer will zero in on any gaps. So, if our teacher really wants the job as the office "lawn man," his application might show him as a member of the school's "maintenance crew" rather than of its teaching staff.

Since you're interested in getting ahead and managing other people, you may have difficulty understanding applicants with this kind of personality. Don't underestimate them. They certainly aren't stupid. They see work from a different perspec-tive than you do. It isn't a matter of who's right and who's wrong. Each attitude is right for the person involved.

It is like the forty-five-year-old CZU dentist who despised

the nineteen-year-old he once was because of the decision to spend the rest of his life looking into people's mouths and filling teeth. There are many unhappy people working at unsuitable jobs and we should respect CZUs for having the courage to change their situation. People resist change, and the combination of resisting change and knowing change is necessary leads to inner emotional conflict. That's what psychologists call avoidance—avoidance conflict: You're trapped by having to choose between two unpleasant alternatives because by doing nothing you're eating yourself alive.

The comfort-zone underachiever is trying to find "what's right for me." The jobs CZUs take may be temporary; they're at a crossroads in a period of reassessment. Often, they're looking for a job that won't divert them from their search. The job will require a minimum of attention, thus freeing them to think, to sort things out. Often, they'll go after a job that's highly repetitive in nature that can be done accurately without effort, thus enabling them to daydream. Certain jobs in your own company would doubtless drive you bananas in two hours, but there are people who enjoy doing those jobs; it's a matter of the proper fit.

Work and Play

The word *work* has a bad image for many people. To them, work is a form of punishment. Perhaps it goes back to the ejection of Adam and Eve from the Garden of Eden. If they had not been driven out, they'd still have had to figure out a way to occupy themselves, but the activities would have been by choice and so would have been thought of as play rather than as work. If a person plays tennis for a living, it's work; but if a person plays it for recreation, it's play. It is still tennis. Perhaps it comes down to a distinction between have-to and want-to situations. That is why many people who are independently wealthy still work. For them, it's a want-to situation.

Describing the Job

In describing a job, you should include some basic information that everybody would like to have, so that they don't have to ask. Tell them the hours, starting salary, length of probationary period, and whether successful completion of the trial period generates a salary increase. You can also include a brief overview of the benefits package. By getting this basic information out of the way, you avoid cluttering up the open-ended questions that provide the attitude clues needed to make a hiring judgment.

Let's return to the sample interview with Mrs. Valencia. In talking with her about the job, describe it in nontechnical terms—use terms she'll understand. The jargon and acronyms of your business may be commonplace to you, but they are a foreign language to new employees. The same situation exists with job descriptions. If they are written in technical jargon, they will mean very little to prospective employees.

Making the Hire

If you're considering several people for the job, be careful not to mislead any of the prospects. Tell them that a decision will not be made until all the prospects have been interviewed. They should appreciate the fairness of that arrangement. Tell them that they will be called as soon as a decision has been reached. See that they are phoned that day and informed of the decision.

At most companies, prospects are phoned by the human resources department and told that a decision has been made. You might, of course, want to deliver the good news yourself and phone the person selected. This approach may make you a big shot with Mrs. Valencia, but it won't do a whole lot for your image with the human resources department: They handle the dirty work; you handle the good news. If they have to inform six people that they didn't get the job, at least let them deliver the good news to the one who is going to be hired.

The Attitude Talk

After the applicant is selected for the job, you should have your "attitude talk" with the person. Following is an example of a good attitude talk. You'll develop your own style after a while, but the basic thoughts remain the same:

> "One of the reasons you were selected for this position is that you display the kind of attitude we want in this organization. Your application and tests indicate that you have the capacity to handle the job. Many of the people who applied had the qualifications to do the job, but the one reason you were selected above all the others was that you display the kind of attitude we are looking for. We believe that the difference between an average employee and an outstanding one is often attitude.
>
> "Not everyone in this organization has a great attitude. What do we mean by *attitude*? The attitude we're talking about is one where you are not worrying about whether you're doing more than your share. It's an attitude of pride in doing high-quality work and gaining a sense of accomplishment at day's end. It's personal satisfaction in a job well done. We believe you display that kind of attitude, and coupled with your ability to handle the job, you will make an outstanding addition to our organization."

Now let's analyze the reasons for some of the statements in this mini-speech.

- When is an employee most likely to be receptive to ideas about the job? Isn't it at the start of a new position?

- Do people generally try to live up to the image they think you have of them? I think they do. Recall the interview and the possibility that the applicant may have been displaying the attitude she thought you wanted. She now knows that attitude is exceedingly important to the company and to you as her manager. She now needs to display such an attitude on the job. Isn't that a win-win situation for both her and the company?

- Why advertise the fact that there are people in the company who do not have a great attitude? If you remain silent about some who may have an undesirable attitude, your words become hollow indeed, when this new employee runs into one of them. However, since you mentioned it, now when she encounters a fellow employee with a bad attitude, your credibility is enhanced. She may think, "He told me there are some with a bad attitude like this. I'm here to help change it." Your credibility is fortified.

The exact timing of your attitude talk with a new employee is a matter of personal preference. Bringing the person back into the office after she has been notified she got the job can be an ideal time to congratulate the person and give the attitude talk. It should be reinforced the first day on the job too, but in a low-key way because there are so many things on the new employee's mind that day. She's nervous; she's concerned about how she's going to like the people she is going to meet and if they will like her. But that first day is when the new employee is most receptive to what is expected.

12

Training Team Members

Many new managers believe they must know how to perform every job in their area of responsibility. It's as though they feel that if some key person quits, they might have to get out there and personally perform the task. If you believe in that philosophy and carry it to its logical conclusion, then the chief executive officer of the organization ought to be able to perform every job in the company. That of course is ridiculous. It's just as ridiculous as believing that the President of the United States should be able to perform every task in the federal government. The President shouldn't even be able to perform every job in the White House. You don't have to be a master chef to recognize rotten chicken.

Your Responsibility for Training

You must know what needs to be done, not exactly how it's done. A lot depends on what level manager you are. If you are a "performer-manager," you are responsible for doing some of the work yourself and leading others in the same function. In that set of circumstances, you will know how to perform the operation.

However, if you have thirty-five people performing a variety of tasks, you will not know how to perform each task—but you will have someone out there who does know how it's done. The administrator of a large hospital is not able to perform surgery, but that administrator knows the process by which skilled surgeons are secured and retained on the staff.

Many new managers are uncomfortable about what they cannot do. Don't be. You're going to be held responsible for the results you achieve within the confines of company policy. You will not be responsible for crossing every *T* and dotting every *I* yourself.

Although this concept may be frightening to you at first, you'll get used to it and wonder how you could have ever thought otherwise. Your initial reaction will be, "I've got to know it all." If it's a big, varied operation, you can't possibly know it all. Don't sweat it.

Training the New Employee

Some jobs require more extensive training than others, but even the most experienced person coming into a new situation needs some basic training. New employees need to be trained as soon as possible in their job, how it is done at your company, and how they fit into the overall organization.

In many ways, instructions given to employees on their first day are wasted motion. Their first day on the job is an opportunity for new employees to become acquainted with the people they'll be working with and to find out where the rest rooms are. You should permit them to spend the first day just observing and then start the actual training the second day. Many workers go home from their first day on the job with either a bad headache or a backache—undoubtedly the result of nervous tension.

There are different philosophies on how a person should be trained. The most common philosophy holds that the person leaving the job should train a new employee. Automatically following that philosophy can be a mistake. Everything depends on why the employee is leaving and on the person's attitude.

Training the Wrong Way: An Example

The following example shows the wrong way to train a new employee. It demonstrates the worst kind of judgment. The manager of an office consisting of several salespeople and one clerical person decided that the clerk should be fired for incompetence. He gave her two weeks' notice but asked her to work during that time. He then hired her replacement and asked her to train the new employee. The result was a nightmare for all concerned.

And no wonder! If the person leaving your company is less than 100 percent competent, you must never allow him to do the training. Why would you want someone fired for incompetence to train her replacement? They're likely to put no effort at all into the training. And even if they do make an effort, they'll probably pass all their bad habits on to the new employee. Even people who are leaving voluntarily usually are not the best trainers. Most people who put in their notice don't give a damn from that point on. The training they do will be casual and incomplete. On the other hand, when a position opens up because the incumbent in the job is being promoted, that person is probably the best one to handle the training.

Concerning the manager who wanted the fired employee to train the replacement, he did not himself understand the clerical job. It was impossible for him personally to train the new employee—any attempt to do so would merely have displayed his ignorance. He therefore went to impossible extremes to "keep his cover." That is a serious managerial failure.

Don't misconstrue this suggestion to mean that a manager must personally know how to perform every job in the organization. In the example given, there was only one clerical operation, so there was no one else available. The manager took the easy route of having the departing clerical worker train the incoming one. Even if he couldn't explain the specific details of the job to the new employee, he should have been able to explain exactly what he expected from the clerical position.

The Role of the Trainer

Before starting a new employee on a training course, you must have a talk with the prospective trainer. You should never spring it as a surprise. Once the new employee is hired and a starting date has been established, notify the person you've selected as the trainer. The trainer may need to rearrange some schedules to accommodate the assignment.

Pick a trainer who is very good at explaining what is going on—one who can break the job down into its component parts and who doesn't describe it in technical jargon. The jargon will be picked up eventually, but this "foreign language" must not overwhelm the trainee.

You must outline to the trainer what you want to happen. If you'd like the first day to be casual, the trainer needs to know that.

Sometime during the latter part of the first day, you should stop by and ask the trainer and the trainee how things are going. What you say is not as important as your display of interest in the new employee.

At the end of the first week, call the employee into the office for a chat. Again, what is said is not as important as the interest displayed in the new employee's welfare. Ask a couple of questions to determine if the instructions from the trainer are clear. Is the new employee beginning to get a handle on the job?

The Improvement Seed

This is also the time for planting the *improvement seed*. The process might take the form of this discussion with the employee:

> "As a new person on this job, you bring fresh insights to the position that the rest of us may not have. After you've been at it a while, you may not be able to see the forest for the trees. I encourage you to ask any questions about what we do and why we do it. After you've been trained, we encourage you to offer any suggestions you can think of to improve what we're doing. Just because you're new doesn't mean your ideas are invalid. What seems obvious to you as a new employee may not be so obvious to the rest of us."

The reason for emphasizing "after you've been at it" is to keep new employees from suggesting changes before they understand what is going on. What may seem like a good idea early in the training may be taken care of as the nature of the position becomes more clearly understood.

Everyone you manage must know that you regularly do this improvement number. In that way, you make it less likely that they'll react negatively to new ideas.

You'll always have plenty of problems with people who defend themselves with the statement, "We've always done it this way." The type of argument is usually desperate; it tells you unmistakably that the person using it can't come up with a valid explanation of why something is being done.

The Job Defined

During the training period, it's a good idea to break the job down into small parts and teach the functions one at a time. In showing new employees the entire function, you run the risk of overwhelming them. Of course, you should explain the purpose of the job first.

Feedback

It's important to develop a method of feedback that lets you know how well the trainee is doing after beginning to work unassisted on the job. The trainee should take over the job from the trainer on a gradual basis as each step in the process is mastered. The feedback method should apply to every employee. The system should be developed in such a manner that unsatisfactory performance always comes to your attention before too much damage is done. The process is vital to your success as a manager, but no strict guidelines can be offered for establishing it because it will vary according to the line of business you're in.

The feedback must be internal. Hearing about the mistake from a dissatisfied client or customer means it is already too late.

You want to correct the problem before the work gets out of your own area of responsibility.

Quality Control

If it is possible to maintain quality control procedures your employees can relate to, so much the better. Don't expect perfection; that's an unrealistic goal. Determine what an acceptable margin of error should be for your area and then strive as a team to reach that goal and eventually better it. The goal must be realistic if you expect the cooperation of your staff.

A baseball player batting .250 can make out extremely well in the major leagues. One batting .300—getting the job done three times out of ten—is now considered a superstar. In business, you can't survive with that kind of percentage. Depending on what kind of business you're in, it's questionable that you could survive even with a 10 percent rate of error. Let's use a 5 percent rate of error for discussion purposes, even though it may not be realistic for your business.

New employees need to know what is expected of them once they're operating on the job alone. If your ultimate goal for them is 95 percent efficiency, it would help them if they knew what your interim targets are. You might expect them to be working at 70 percent efficiency at the end of thirty days, at 80 percent efficiency at the end of sixty days, and at 95 percent efficiency at the end of ninety days. This will depend on how difficult the work is. The simpler the job, the easier it should be to get to the ultimate quality goal. You need to determine the timetable and let the new employee know what it is.

Even when the new employees take over the job on their own, you should have the trainer audit their work until you believe the work is acceptable and quality checks are not as crucial.

Each mistake should be gone over carefully with the trainee. The trainer must be a diplomat. The trainer must talk about what went wrong and not attack the new employee. Don't make it personal. The trainer should not say, "You're making a mistake again." Rather, something like this might be more appropriate: "Well, this still is not 100 percent, but I think we're getting closer, don't you?"

End of the Training Period

At some point the probationary period must end. In most companies, this is usually after a specified number of weeks or months. However, once the trainee demonstrates the ability to work unassisted, it's time for another formal interview between you and the trainee. This marks the completion of a phase in the new employee's career, and some attention should be paid to the event. All you really need to do is express your satisfaction about the progress made up to this point, note that the employee will now be working on his or her own, and indicate how the work will be monitored both for quality and quantity.

13

Managing Change: Dealing with Resistance

One of the most important aspects of a manager's job is managing change effectively. Managing change includes accepting change and supporting it, understanding why your team members may be resistant to it, and finding ways to reduce that resistance. When you are able to do all three of these, you have mastered one of the most critical competencies of any manager.

Accept Change Yourself

Have you ever worked for a manager who found it difficult to accept the changes that the organization had initiated? This type of manager will openly express disagreement, call the decision makers fools who have no clue what they are doing, and try to convince you that most of these changes were terrible for the staff as well. This is a terrible mistake on the part of a manager. It causes employees to lose faith in company decisions and, ultimately, in the company.

As a manager, not only do you have to be prepared to embrace change and be a champion of it but also to accept and support changes that the company has decided upon, even if you disagree with the change. It is best to admit that you do not like the change (as your staff may already know this), but state that you will actively support it and expect your staff to support it as well.

For example, let's say that the company has decided to go with a new computer system. And let's say that you feel the old system is currently giving you what you need. What would be the danger of not supporting the new decision? First, you are only looking at the change from your vantage point and the benefits you do not see may not be real for others in the company. Second, you are sending a message that your opinion counts more than that of the organization. It is important as a new manager that you get your team to align themselves with the goals and decisions of the organization. Ideally, it would be best if you were part of the decision-making process and upper management asked your thoughts and listened to your opinions. Then, perhaps, you could accept the change more readily, even if you disagreed with it. But, unfortunately, even if they do not include you in the decision-making process, as a manager, you must actively communicate your support for company policies, procedures, rules, regulations, and decisions.

Resistance to Change

Most people are naturally resistant to change. There is often resistance even when an apparently good change is introduced in the workplace. What makes people so resistant to change? People basically fear the unknown and how they will react to uncertainties. In today's economy, a change may mean a loss of a job. Many may believe they do not have the skills to perform the responsibilities that the change may bring or they are unclear about the reasons why the change is being introduced in the first place.

Resistance to change is also very subjective. That is, people have different threshold levels to change. Some of us who have had bad experiences with change, or grew up in environments where change was a dirty word, will obviously be much more resistant when change occurs than those who have benefited from change in the past, or were taught early on to embrace change. Resistance to change is subjective in another way. There are certain changes that affect people in different ways. For example, Mary has always prepared documentation for any package she sends out so that she will be able to track it later on if necessary, or quickly answer any questions from customers, vendors, salespeople, and so forth. Fran has never done this; she thinks it is a waste of her time. When the company institutes a new policy calling for careful documentation of all outgoing packages, Mary is unfazed. Fran reacts negatively to this new "busywork" and complains to everybody she can about it.

How to Reduce Resistance

It is unwise to think that you can totally eliminate your team's resistance to workplace changes. As we said, people will normally be resistant. You will be more successful if you try to reduce the amount of resistance. The best strategy is to involve your employees in the change.

First, explain why the change is occurring and point out any benefits to them. Often there are no benefits for them. The customer may benefit or some other department may flourish as a result. Sometimes, you just have to be honest and say something like "We will still be in business" or "You will still have a job."

Then, ask their thoughts on how the change can be implemented in their group or your department. The more you involve others with the change the more readily they seem to accept it. Sometimes your most resistant employees, once involved, become your biggest champions for the change. Always try to identify the most resistant individuals from the beginning and get them on your side. Change occurs so much more easily when you have their support.

14

Disciplining the Employee

Performance standards vary by the kind of business you are in, and may even vary by departments within the same company, because of the variety of tasks involved.

Every employee you are managing must know what work standards are expected. You create nasty problems for yourself when you discipline an employee on the basis of vague work standards. (It's like the way some people describe a tasteless movie: "Well, I can't define it, but I know it when I see it.") You can't get by with a nebulous approach to performance standards.

Let's assume you've done a satisfactory job of establishing standards for each job. In all probability, those standards are written into a job description. The job description indicates the elements of accountability that apply to the job; you can therefore measure the individual against those standards. Now you must have methods within your area of responsibility that allow you to be constantly aware of how people are performing in relationship to the standards. You cannot operate on the assumption that unless you're hearing complaints from customers, or other departments, the performance is acceptable. By the time such warning signals arrive, severe damage may already have been done.

Prior Knowledge

Your own attitude about performance is crucial. The place and time for conveying your attitude about performance to employees is when they first step into the job. They need to know exactly what is expected of them. Performance standards will change. During the training period, you'll accept less in the way of quality and quantity than afterward. You should have this properly backstopped during the training period so that the trainee's errors don't reach beyond your own department.

Feedback is critical to proper and effective discipline. You must know as soon as possible when performance is substandard so that it can be corrected immediately. In the following discussion of discipline procedures, let's assume that you've set adequate standards and that the employee knows what those standards are. Furthermore, you have an adequate method of feedback so that you know when substandard performance is a problem.

Never Make It Personal

One of the oldest rules of management is that employee discipline should always be done in private. Never humiliate an employee, even in cases of dismissal. The employee must always be made to understand that what is being discussed is the performance, not the person.

Too many managers, at all levels of experience, turn a discussion of poor performance into a personal attack. In most cases, it's probably not done maliciously. This kind of approach is simply not thought through.

The following opening gambits often get the discussion off to a terrible start:

"You are making far too many errors."

"I don't know what your problem is. I've never had anyone screw up on this job like you."

"Your performance is so substandard that we don't have an
  adjective to describe it."

These are outrageous statements, but attacks like these are
uttered every working day somewhere. The managers may feel
that they are right on target, but they have just made their problems worse than they need to be.

Employees feel that they are being personally attacked.
When attacked, our natural tendency is to defend ourselves, and
the defensive barriers of these employees go up. Now both parties to the conversation have to fight through these barriers to
get back to the problem. Give employees the benefit of the
doubt. You might say, "I know you are concerned about the
quality of the work at your desk." Attack the substandard performance by viewing it as the result of some misunderstanding
about how the work should be done. Perhaps the employee has
missed something in the training process, and this has created a
systems deficiency that is causing the work to fall below the
company's standards. By taking this approach, you inform the
employee from the outset that you're talking about the performance and not the person.

Give and Take

You should have a conversation, not deliver a monologue. Many
managers do all the talking, meanwhile building up resentment
in the party on the receiving end. You need to encourage the
employee's participation in the conversation. Without it there is
a good chance you won't solve the problem.

Be careful, now, and don't go overboard! Some executives,
in their effort to be scrupulously fair, become so cautious and
tactful that the employee leaves their office expecting to get a
raise for outstanding performance. You have to make certain that
your direct report understands that the work is not up to standards. How you say it, though, is critically important.

When bringing the employee into your office, put him or
her at ease. This may not seem like a big thing to you, but to an
employee, who doesn't often enter the sanctum of the high and

mighty, you're the boss and being called into your presence may be a frightening prospect. Therefore, do everything you can to make the other person comfortable.

Encourage the employee to participate in the discussion early in the game. You might start off with a statement like this: "Fred, you've been with us three months now and I think it's time we had a conversation about how you're getting along. As you know, I have a great interest in your being successful on this job. How do you feel things are going?"

By using this approach, you encourage an employee who is not performing up to standards to bring up the subject himself. It seldom comes as a surprise to an employee to learn that specified standards are not being met. Surprise is likely only if the employee has never been told what is expected. If that is the case, you really have some serious problems—problems of training and communication.

As the employee describes how things are going, you direct the conversation to the standards that are not being met. For example, you ask, "Do you think you're getting close to the standards we've established for experienced employees?" If the answer is yes, you could ask, "Do you believe you're performing at the same level as an experienced employee?" If the answer is again yes, then the employee may be out of touch with reality. The point is to continue asking questions of this type until you get the kind of response that will lead you into a discussion of the quality of the work.

Obviously, if all your tactful efforts have failed to induce the employee to bring up the crucial subject, you have no choice but to insert it into the conversation yourself. To the employee who persists in asserting that things are going well, you could say, "That's an interesting observation you've made about the quality of the work, because my observation indicates that it's not up to the standards we've set for the job. Why do you suppose my information is different from yours?" You then have the matter out on the desk for discussion.

Eliminate Misunderstanding

As you proceed further into the conversation, you use techniques that ensure the employee knows what's expected. It's a good idea to get feedback on what you've mutually agreed upon, so there can be no misunderstanding later about what was said.

One way to make certain of this is to write a memorandum at the conclusion of the conversation and place it in the employee's file. This becomes particularly important if you are managing a lot of people and it's possible that six months from now you won't remember the details of the conversation.

The Primacy of the Person

There are problems about an employee's performance that cannot be separated from the person. When talking about the quality or quantity of an employee's work, it's obvious that the techniques discussed in this chapter can help in establishing firmly in the employee's mind that a difference exists between your criticism of the work and your view of the person. But with certain attitudinal problems, it's more difficult to make the distinction, and in many cases it can't be done.

Let's assume you have a highly satisfactory employee who can't seem to get to work on time. Disciplining unsatisfactory employees is easier than disciplining a problem employee like this one whom you obviously want to keep. What happens in these situations is that if you allow the employee the privilege of coming in late every day, you're going to create a morale problem with the rest of the people who adhere to the office hours, no matter how superior that person's performance is. (This obviously does not apply if your office has flexible working hours.)

In talking with the satisfactory employee about this problem, one of the better approaches is to explain the management difficulties you'd have if every employee ignored the working hours. You couldn't tolerate that situation. In addition, the employee is creating difficulties for himself. You can then go into the discussion in some detail and start working on a solution. Let's follow through with this problem of the tardy employee, because it happens often enough that you'll eventually have to face it.

Most conscientious employees who are doing a satisfactory job will react positively to your statements. You may notice that for the next ten days or so they appear at their desks on time. At that point, you'll be feeling pretty smug about your success in managing people. You'll find, however, that when the pressure is off, the reformed employees will be coming in late again. You can't take a casual approach about this and assume it was just an unusual set of circumstances. All your subordinates must be made to know you expect them to be on time every day.

The first time this happens after your initial conversation, you again have a discussion with the offender. This doesn't have to be a full-blown dialogue of the same length and detail as the first one. All you need to do is reinforce what you said previously. There may have been a sound reason for the latest time abuse, and it could be that the second conversation will keep the employee on the straight and narrow. If you can get to the point where the employee is coming to work on time for approximately six months, you may assume you've changed that person's work patterns enough so that you no longer have a serious problem. What you should expect from that point on is the same attendance as you get from the rest of your employees.

Discipline for a Good Employee Gone Bad

Let's look at a step-by-step case study regarding the use of employee time that is as challenging an employee-disciplinary situation as you are likely to face. Kelly, one of your direct reports, does executive coaching for your consulting firm. She goes to client sites and works with senior managers, one on one, helping them with their managerial skills, computer skills, and giving advice on project implementation. She usually spends one day a week at a client site for a month or two. You have always gotten the best feedback from the clients about Kelly. She is always in high demand. You consider her to be your best staff member.

Then, the table suddenly starts to turn. You begin to receive feedback from these same clients, and new ones, that her short breaks of five or ten minutes are turning into an hour or more a couple times a day, and these breaks are not during lunch. After a couple weeks of listening to these comments, you set up a meeting with Kelly and tell her of the complaints you are getting about her. You explain that it makes both her and your company look unprofessional when she leaves one of these senior executives hanging and that these client companies are paying big bucks for your services. You also explain that the executives have scheduled their day around her being there.

Kelly doesn't believe she is taking such long breaks and flatly denies it. You try to open the floor to her and have her discuss anything that is troubling her, work-wise or personally, but she just keeps saying that everything is perfect and that she cannot imagine that she is taking such long breaks. You decide on an action plan. Kelly will notify the client when she needs five or ten minutes (she's a smoker), look at her watch, tell the client what time it is and what time she will return.

You think the problem is over. But it isn't. You continue to receive the same complaints from clients, so you have a couple of additional discipline sessions with Kelly. They lead nowhere. You even suggest that Kelly visit an outside counselor, at company expense, if she wants or needs to talk to someone. She refuses your offer. The same behavior continues. You give her one last opportunity to change. You tell her if you get one more complaint on the same issue she will be gone. You get several more and Kelly is terminated.

The situation just described is one that many people would view as a failure of management skills. That's wrong. Not every personnel problem can be solved by accommodation. In the case study described here, you did everything you could to remedy the situation. You gave Kelly every opportunity to address her behavior, to open up to you concerning whatever problems she may have, you worked out a plan for her to follow, and you gave her several chances to change her behavior. Since nothing you did worked, the only solution you had was to get someone to replace her, no matter how valuable an employee she had been at one time.

Other Problems

It's possible and probable that you'll have other problems of a similar nature, such as spending too much time on the Internet for non-work-related activities, consistently overstaying the lunch hour, or just failing to show up. Needless to say, you don't run a sweatshop, and everyone will occasionally have some issue at one time or other. What is critical is dealing effectively with chronic offenders who create management problems for you and the organization.

Another difficult problem that is among the most challenging for a manager to handle is personal hygiene. For example, suppose you have a young woman in your department who has an unpleasant body odor. Other employees are making sly comments about her. Even worse, they are avoiding her. This is unacceptable because their work depends on communicating with her often during the day. Her body odor has become a business issue and so you have to speak to her about it.

Rather than do it yourself, you may want to arrange to have someone in human resources talk directly to the employee. The reason would not be to avoid a difficult situation, but rather to spare the woman embarrassment every time she saw you and the misery of being constantly reminded of the uncomfortable conversation. By having someone in human resources talk to her away from her work area, you might solve the problem and also be able to salvage an otherwise satisfactory employee. If the embarrassment is too great in a delicate situation like this, you may lose the employee.

Disciplinary Techniques

You have a highly satisfactory employee whose work sharply deteriorates. Needless to say, you're continually communicating with the employee about the deterioration. You want to retain the employee, but you find that your words are not being taken seriously. In a situation like this one, you may recommend zero salary increase for the employee for that year, with a full explanation as to why you're doing it. Inform the employee in advance that if the work doesn't get better, there'll be no increase in pay. Having made that threat or stated that possibility of action, you must then follow through on it so that you don't lose credibility. Some people don't actually believe you'll take such action. It's a technique that frequently works because people still care about the paycheck.

Another disciplinary technique you can use is to put the employee on probation. State that the person's work deterioration needs to be corrected, and you want to give the employee every opportunity to correct it. You must make it perfectly clear that the substandard level of work being delivered cannot be allowed to continue. Also, you should set a deadline for a resolution to the problem. You might say to the employee, "This problem has to be solved within one month or we'll have to make other arrangements."

But first, the employee must be made to understand exactly what kind of performance is being labeled substandard. The employee must also know how to correct it and must know what level of performance is expected. You must not arrive at the end of the probationary period only to find a legitimate difference of opinion as to how the employee is performing. The standards must be set so clearly that no disagreement about whether they've been met or not is possible. They must be measurable standards. You must keep a satisfactory set of records, because you may have to justify firing the employee if it comes to that.

Records are also helpful in raising performance standards. You can use the records to show your direct reports how they improved the quality of their work. This becomes an added gain because the employees are inspired to greater effort by pride in their accomplishment.

New employees in a company are often put on probation, either in line with standard company policy or as individual cases. You cannot establish a probationary period for every employee in your department or division if it's not a company-wide practice. Many companies use a ninety-day probationary period. Employees doing satisfactory work at the end of that time are taken off the probationary rolls and become regular employees. It's also customary to give a modest salary increase in recognition of satisfactory completion of the probationary course. If the work is not satisfactory at that point, the employee should anticipate being terminated. Again, it should never come as a surprise.

15

"Oh My God!
I Can't Fire Anyone!"

If there's one moment that will live forever in a manager's memory, it's the first time a direct report must be fired. It's not a pleasant task. If you enjoy it, there is something terribly wrong with your ability to manage people.

Firing someone can be traumatic for both parties in the drama. If you've done your job properly, the event will not come as a surprise to the person who is about to get the ax.

Sudden firings are nearly always wrong, except in cases where an employee has been dishonest or violent. Most companies have strict guidelines as to what offenses call for immediate dismissal. Never fire someone when you're angry. Never take such radical action on an impulse. When a direct report pushes you over the edge and you feel like "showing who's boss," don't give in to your emotions. If you do, you'll regret it.

As you read this chapter, the thought may occur to you that some people don't deserve the time and consideration that it takes to terminate someone. Once again, most companies have guidelines on the termination process. Ask your manager or HR if you are not sure what they are. It is best to err on the side of excess deliberation rather than on the side of excess haste. In fact, some managers adopt the philosophy of never firing a direct report until everyone in the office is wondering why they haven't taken the step already. They may be a little extreme.

Prepare the Grounds for the Divorce

Documentation of the troublesome employee's performance is critically important. Of course, you must keep these records for all your employees. If your company has a formal performance appraisal system, then you may be adequately covered.

Records are important because being sued for dismissing an employee is becoming more common. You should ask yourself, "If I have to, can I fully justify this dismissal?" If you can answer yes, that's all you need worry about.

Many managers agonize over every situation where they've had to let someone go. It is better that a manager care too much than to be completely callous about it.

The more typical kinds of discharge that you're likely to run into in your managerial career have to do with poor performance and the employee's inability or unwillingness to abide by the company's standards. Some people will never be able to cut the job. They may get to a satisfactory training performance level but will never advance beyond that point to the performance level the job requires.

Firing is not the first thought that should come into your head. You must first satisfy yourself that the training has been correct and clearly understood. Was there any kind of personality barrier between the trainer and the trainee that impeded the flow of adequate information? Go back over the employee's aptitude tests, job application, and other initial hiring data on the chance that you may have missed something. Only after you are completely convinced that you have a below-satisfactory performer with little or no hope of bringing the performance up to proper standards should you consider termination as a possible solution.

Has the new employee been told that his or her performance is not up to the standard that is expected? You owe it to your people to let them know what the situation is. And that includes telling them when they're performing well. Too many managers assume that if employees don't get bad performance reports, they know they're doing okay. This is usually not the case. Those employees tend to believe you "don't give a damn."

Mergers and Buyouts

We have been seeing an onslaught of mergers and buyouts. Usually, everyone is told that the new corporation is planning on no personnel changes, but within six months, the personnel changes begin. Reorganization takes place and some people are fired. After a corporate takeover, everyone is scrambling to protect his or her own position. Some people survive and some don't. Those who do not survive are not necessarily inadequate. They may be filling positions that are duplicated in the parent organization. Some people are fired because they are too high in the organization or because their salary is too high.

If you become involved in one of these takeovers, you can only hope that the parent corporation is humane. If it is necessary to let some people go, it should be done in a way that acknowledges responsibility to these human beings. Continuing their salary for a reasonable length of time, providing office space and secretarial help while they look for a new position, and personal counseling are some methods used to soften the blow.

It is doubtful that you as manager will have anything new to tell employees about the takeover. You may get saddled with the job of telling some people in your area that they are being let go. It may even be possible that you have to select the people who are to be let go. You may have been told to reduce staff by 10 percent or reduce salary costs by 20 percent. These are difficult decisions because they often have little to do with performance. All you can do is carry out the task in as humane a manner as possible. Everyone knows the staff reduction is a result of the merger, so you might as well tie it to that; it at least allows people to save face. If they can't save their job, saving face is some consolation. Use whatever influence you have with the organization to generate some help for these people.

Seniority is often a poor way to pick employees to be let go, but that's how many companies operate in the interest of "fairness" (and to avoid being sued). If the last people hired are the first fired, at least none of them can complain that such a system is personal.

Downsizing

Downsizing is a word that strikes fear in employee groups. We won't get into all the controversy over downsizing, except to say that it does not always achieve the desired results. We'll discuss two basic elements: your survival as an employee and the role you might be required to play as a new manager.

Your boss is going to be worried about his or her own survival and looking at your area of responsibility. The downsizing tremor is felt through the entire organization. Many managers and executives who thought they were immune from the downsizing virus end up being totally shocked.

The best advice is, "Don't let them see you sweat." Have confidence in your ability. Instead of going into your boss's office and trying to find out what your prospects are for survival, take a different approach. Asking about your survival is just another problem piled on your manager. Why not say, "I know that this is going to be a difficult time for you. I want you to know that I'm here to help you any way I can."

No one can guarantee your survival in a downsizing operation, but you may increase the odds if you are a part of the solution rather than whining about your own job and putting an additional burden on your manager's shoulders.

As a manager, you may end up giving some bad news to people who are losing their jobs. The comments earlier under "Mergers and Buyouts" also apply to this section as a humane way to handle these personal contacts.

Let's hope that the organization you are a part of is a humane one that provides some help to people who are losing their jobs, with items such as salary continuance, continuation of health coverage for a reasonable length of time, and major assistance in helping find another job.

Even if you survive the downsizing, it's difficult to feel great about your good fortune when many of your friends did not fare as well. You may even feel a bit guilty about your survival, and that is a perfectly natural reaction for a humane manager.

A Second Chance

When an employee's job performance is unsatisfactory, it is important to make clear in your discussion with the employee that you're addressing yourself to the work and not to the person. At some point in the conversation, you let the employee know that termination will come if the performance standards cannot be met. But it's not enough to let it go at that. Set a target for the employee to reach, in terms of both work improvement and time to achieve the goal. You need to be specific: "The average daily errors are five. We need to cut that down to three errors per day by the end of the month." Your precise specifications serve a dual purpose. If the employee meets the goal, you may be on the way to solving the problem *and* retaining the employee. Failing that, you're ready to start the termination process.

Here are some key questions to ask yourself before taking the final step of termination:

- Is it possible that this employee could handle some other job in your own area that is currently available?
- If an opening is coming up in another area, can the employee make a contribution there?
- Is this a situation where a person has been hired for the wrong job? Does the company gain anything by firing someone who might be useful somewhere else?
- Will the employee be so embarrassed by what appears to be failure that the stigma will carry over into future jobs?
- Is your company large enough that the employee could be moved to another area with no stigma?
- Former employees are part of a company's public. Can you handle the situation in such a way that you don't deplete your company's storehouse of civic goodwill?

- Even though the employee won't like being fired, can you handle the procedure so that the employee will admit to having been given every opportunity and will consequently agree that you had no choice in the matter?

Listen to this warning against taking the coward's way out and blaming the mysterious *they*. "As far as I'm concerned, five errors a day isn't too bad, but *they* say we have to get it down to three, or *they* will force me to let you go." That indicates you're merely a puppet. Someone else is pulling the strings. You don't have a mind of your own.

You have to level with the employee who is not measuring up. I know of managers who sugarcoat all bad news to such an extent that the employee on the receiving end feels complimented on having done an outstanding job.

Flexibility and Consistency

Some of your people will also need to be dismissed because of excessive absenteeism. Companies have such a wide variety of sick-leave programs, however, that it's impossible to discuss what level of absenteeism is satisfactory. Some companies have fixed programs that allow, for example, one sick day per month or twelve per year, cumulatively. Other companies have a method that allows managerial discretion based on the individual situation. Admittedly, this kind of program is more difficult to administer than one with hard-and-fast rules to follow. In evaluating the merits of each case, you must be able to defend your decision.

One disadvantage in having no formal program is the serious risk that decisions will not be made consistently throughout the company. For example, generous managers may be inclined to excuse almost any absence and pay the absentee; other managers may be stricter and dock for days missed. Having no formal program means the communication between departments and managers has to be extremely good, ensuring that approximately the same standards apply throughout the company.

The Dismissal Drama

So far we've discussed events leading up to a dismissal. Now let's talk about the dismissal itself. Let's focus on the dismissal whose timing you control.

Most managers like to stage the drama late Friday afternoon. By the time it's over, all the coworkers of the person being fired have left the office. Thus, the dismissed employee won't have to endure the humiliation of "clearing out" in front of an audience. Also, the employee can use the weekend to pull things together and prepare for seeking other employment, applying for unemployment compensation, or doing whatever else needs to be done.

Any money due at the time of the dismissal should be given to the dismissed employee at the end of the interview. Being canned is enough of an emotional blow; wondering when the final check will arrive can only add to the misery. Severance pay—if that's the company's policy—should be given at the same time. Unused vacation time or sick leave should also be included in the compensation.

Put yourself in the other person's position. You're not going to feel the termination was completely justified. Unless you receive every dollar you have coming to you, you'll probably think, "Well, I suppose I'll have to hire an attorney to get the money this chicken outfit owes me!" Remove that thought from the dismissed employee's mind by taking care of all those matters in advance.

Another courtesy that is owed to the employee is to keep your intention to fire him or her as confidential as possible. Of course, the human resources and the payroll departments will have to know. But other than discussing it with the necessary management people, you should treat the matter confidentially.

The final scene in the dismissal drama is bound to be most uncomfortable for you, the manager. This is because in that highly charged final interview, it's just the two of you face-to-face, and you want to get it over with as quickly as possible.

A good way to start the dismissal or termination interview

is to review in brief what has happened. Don't drag it out and make it a recitation of all the other person's mistakes. It should go something like this:

> "As you know from our past conversations, we had certain standards on the job that had to be met. I think we approached reaching those standards on a fair and reasonable basis. As I've mentioned to you from time to time over the past few weeks, the work is not up to those standards. I don't believe it's because of any lack of effort on your part. However, it hasn't worked out, and I don't think that comes as any surprise to you. We're going to have to terminate your services as of today. I really regret that. I wanted it to work out just as much as you did. But it hasn't worked out, and so we have to face up to reality. Here's the final check, including one month's severance pay plus your unused vacation and sick-leave time. This should give you a continuation of income for a time sufficient for you to find another job."

You can vary your remarks to fit the individual situation, but the above words say what needs to be said. They don't sugarcoat the bad news and they're not too blunt either. You have to come up with a statement that fits the situation, and one you're comfortable with.

Fortunately, the days of putting a pink slip in someone's pay envelope are gone. That practice was highly inhumane. One can understand the necessity for it in a factory where thousands of people are all being temporarily laid off or where the entire business is being closed and everybody is going. Situations like that are not related to the performance of the individual. When someone is being let go because of a failure to perform or live up to company standards, the only way to handle it is on a one-on-one basis. As manager, you might prefer to avoid the direct confrontation, but it's part of the job's responsibilities and must be dealt with straight on. In most companies, this final interview is the last step in the disciplinary procedure and under employment law it is considered the appropriate thing to do.

Last Thoughts on Firing

When you consider it thoughtfully, you realize that keeping an unsatisfactory employee on the job is unfair not only to the company but also to the employee. No one is comfortable in a job he is not performing well.

There are many instances where being fired has turned out to be the biggest favor a company can do for an employee who isn't suited for his or her job. It may not seem that way to the employee at the time, but later on, she'll know it was the right thing and that she actually came out ahead in the long run. Consider the following true story:

A young man just out of a community college was trying to function in an accounting position but was not cutting the mustard. After being let go, he decided to continue his education. He got his bachelor's degree and then was accepted into law school and graduated near the top of his class. To make a long story short, he is now practicing his profession very successfully. In fact, he is the head of the law department managing a staff of thirty lawyers in that same company that fired him fifteen years earlier.

Some managers feel like failures if they have to fire anyone. This statistic may help you out. Research on employee termination has shown that seven out of ten people who get dismissed do better on their next job, both in both performance and salary. Their former job was a poor fit. They have found a better fit for themselves.

People seem to avoid the word *fire* as they do the word *die.* Instead of *die,* they say *pass away, go on to his reward,* or *cross over.* Instead of *fire,* they say *dismiss, discharge, let go, can.* There should be nothing wrong with saying the words *fire* or *terminate.*

Let's end on the most important point in this chapter. You must be absolutely certain in your own mind that the firing is deserved. You must be sure you're being as objective as you can possibly be. If in doubt, use a more experienced manager or HR as a sounding board. Then when you know you have to fire the employee, make sure it doesn't come as a surprise. And handle it in a considerate, humane, and delicate manner.

16

Having a Legal Awareness

It is very important as a first-time manager that you know current employment laws, practices, and regulations set by federal, state, and local governments in order to avoid any legal liability. You do not need to be an expert. That is the job of human resources. When in doubt about what you can and cannot do, or if you are not sure, for example, what constitutes sexual harassment in the workplace, you need to find out.

It would be to your benefit to have a brief overview of the main legal pitfalls that new managers need to avoid and what your legal responsibilities are as a manager. You need to focus on the legal issues around sexual harassment, disability, substance abuse, privacy, family and medical leave, and workplace violence. Once again, you do not have to be the legal expert here. However, under the eyes of the law, ignorance is not an acceptable excuse. Far too many companies are sued and have to pay out huge sums of money because their managers were ignorant of the laws and/or did nothing to enforce them.

Sexual Harassment

Sexual harassment occurs whenever unwelcome behavior on the basis of gender impacts an individual's job. According to the

Equal Employment Opportunity Commission, sexual harassment is defined as unwelcome sexual advances, requests for sexual favors, and other verbal or physical conduct of a sexual nature that interferes with an individual's work performance or creates a hostile or offensive working environment.

Any organization is liable for being a hostile environment, unless the organization can show it acted to prevent and correct sexually harassing behavior. Basically, what that means is if you allow or do not recognize or do nothing about sexual harassment in your department, the company is legally liable. And you can be sure they will not be too happy with you!

Danger Signs

To help you out in preventing and being aware of sexual harassment in your work environments, you should be aware of the following danger signs:

- Telling sexual jokes
- Making kissing sounds
- Discussing sexual topics
- Calling a work colleague "sweetie" or "hot" or "baby"
- Making derogatory comments about one of the genders
- Having inappropriate pictures hanging up in the office or worn on clothing or even on coffee mugs or drinking glasses
- Any form of touching that another person feels is inappropriate (even shaking someone's hand inappropriately)
- Assigning less important responsibilities to members of one gender
- Not giving promotional opportunities equally to all staff members
- Giving individuals preferential treatment because of their gender

As you see this list of danger signs, sexual harassment can be obvious behavior or it can also occur in a more subtle way.

Most organizations today have training classes on what sexual harassment means and how to prevent it in the workplace. Many other organizations have their employees take a short online course and then have them state that they have read the information and will abide by it. They may also be given a test. Taking the test and having staff sign off on it shows the government that the company has made every effort to educate its staff. As a manager, you need to do everything in your control to make sure your staff understands that sexual harassment is not tolerated in any form whatsoever. And as a manager, you must report any incidences of sexually harassment immediately. If you avoid doing so, you and your organization are liable.

Disability

The term *disability* means having a physical or mental impairment that significantly prevents an individual from performing one or more of life's activities or having such a record of impairment. The Americans with Disabilities Act (ADA) bars discrimination against the disabled. You are allowed to tell a job applicant (you have to do it for all job applicants for the same position) that the job has certain physical or mental requirements, and ask the applicant if he or she is willing and able to perform those duties. Most companies today make every effort to accommodate the needs of the disabled.

It is imperative that your department is free of any discrimination or harassment of the disabled. The following example concerns discrimination based on disability. In a local branch of a large banking organization, two employees, both bank clerks, were candidates for promotion to branch manager. They had equivalent banking skills, tenure, performance reviews, and so forth. However, one of the candidates, Henry, was really great in customer service. Customers would always remark how helpful and professional Henry was. So you might be thinking that Henry got the job because he had an edge over the other candidate, Marcia. Wrong. He did not get the job because he was disabled.

The current branch manager making the hiring decision used the following reasoning. She said that an important part of the job was the socializing that took place after work and weekends with the branch manager and the staff. Quite often, these activities were physical in nature—rafting, bike riding, volleyball, and so forth. Since Henry could not participate in these activities, the branch manager decided to promote Marcia. You won't be surprised to learn that Henry filed a nice big lawsuit and won.

Substance Abuse

Most companies have employee handbooks. Usually in those handbooks is a list of behaviors, if committed by an employee on work premises, that are cause for immediate dismissal. Using drugs or alcohol are on the top of that list. However, drug and alcohol abusers are considered to be physically handicapped under the Federal Rehabilitation Act of 1973 and are thereby protected from discrimination. As a manager, you must be aware of the following.

First, you cannot accuse someone of being intoxicated or on drugs. You can ask an employee if she has been drinking or abusing drugs. If the employee denies it, you are legally required to describe the symptoms that led you to ask the question in the first place. The symptoms may be sleeping on the job, slurring words, banging into furniture or equipment, productivity or quality issues, and so forth. Your best bet is to focus only on the employee's behavior. If the employee does not have a good reason for behaving that way, you are permitted to send the employee home for his or her safety and/or the safety of others. If you do this, do not allow the person to drive home on his or her own. You and the company are legally responsible if something happens to the employee or if they person causes an accident on the way home.

Second, do not share information about employees who

have suspected drug or alcohol problems. This could be the cause of a lawsuit for defaming character. The only individuals who you would want to share such information with are your manager, human resources, or a qualified counselor.

Third, you and the organization have the responsibility under most state laws of finding avenues for an employee's rehabilitation. You must try to get the employee to an employee assistance program professional. This person can give the employee the right guidance. If the person's behavior does not improve and the person is not enrolled in a rehabilitation program, you can begin disciplinary procedures.

Privacy

Most companies have the legal right to inspect an employee's work area, listen to voice mails, or look at e-mails and computer files, if they feel they have just cause. Nevertheless, privacy is a right guaranteed by the U.S. Constitution and most state constitutions. Therefore, you need to find out what information about an employee you can and cannot disclose to other parties. For example, you cannot disclose drug test results, payroll information, or credit information such as consumer loans. On the other hand, you can give references to a future employer. But in most companies these days, a signed statement from the past employee is needed.

Family and Medical Leave

The Family and Medical Leave Act (FMLA) permits employees to take unpaid leave for up to three months per year. Currently, the law only holds for organizations with fifty or more employees. Employees can apply for leave for the birth or care of a baby, care of another child or a spouse or a close relative, or if employees have health issues of their own. Under law, an employee's job position or a similar position is guaranteed upon their return. Employees are also entitled to receive all their health benefits while on family leave. An employee must have worked for an organization for approximately twelve months before he or she is eligible to apply. There are many other specifics to the law that your human resources team will know.

Violence in the Workplace

Statistics are showing that violence in the workplace is on the rise and this should be a concern for every organization and manager. Examples of workplace violence include threats, verbal abuse, bullying, shoving, pushing, passive-aggressive behavior such as going into the computer system and causing it problems, and use of a dangerous or lethal weapon.

Every organization and manager needs to demonstrate that they are doing everything possible to maintain an environment free of violence. The following warning signs can signal that your department or organization might be predisposed to violence:

- Employees have no or little opportunity for their views to be heard.
- Training is not provided to develop new skills.
- Poor supervision—studies have shown that this is the number one cause of increased levels of violence at work. The violence is often directed at the bad manager.
- Lack of respect for employees at any level.
- Employees who have a history of workplace violence.
- Employees who are having severe personal problems.
- Substance abuse.
- Employees who undergo significant changes in their appearance, interpersonal communication, and other behaviors.
- An environment that encourages fierce competition between employees or groups of employees resulting in individuals feeling like they are losers.

- A security system that does not do an adequate job of screening "outsiders."

If you have to deal personally with a violent individual within your own department, try to stay calm, use nonthreatening language, try to keep the person talking, and alert company security.

The Manager's Role

You have the crucial and critical role in establishing and maintaining a safe and respectful workplace. It is one of your most important managerial responsibilities. It is also a legal responsibility. Remember, when you are not sure what to do in any of the areas discussed in this chapter, contact someone who does.

PART THREE

WORKING WITH PEOPLE
AND BUILDING
RELATIONSHIPS

17

No Secrets

Too many managers, both first-time and long-time, take some private pleasure in knowing something that others do not know. They assume that if you don't give others certain information, they don't know about it. That is an incorrect conclusion. If people don't know what is going on, they simply assume what is going on. What is worse, they may assume something that is not so, and even worse than that, they may act upon those incorrect assumptions.

There are some bad managers out there who do not like to share information with their direct reports. They believe that if they keep information to themselves, they will be more powerful. They have it all wrong, though. The most powerful managers are those who share information with their direct reports, thereby giving the latter the power to become self-directed.

You've probably heard this before—and it's an important fact for managers to be constantly aware of—people don't act upon the facts; they act upon their perception of the facts. It is one of the manager's key duties to see that the facts and the perceptions are basically the same.

Very little that goes on in an organization needs to be secret. Oftentimes, the things that are secret are merely a matter of timing: "We need to sit on this for a couple of weeks until the details are worked out."

The delight some managers feel in holding unnecessary secrets from staff is potential trouble, however. If people's assumptions about what was discussed at a managers' meeting
are incorrect, and they act upon those false assumptions, you
build your managerial career on a foundation of rotten timbers.
It is more difficult to correct people's knowledge of what is *not*
so than it is to let them know what *is so* in the first place.

A Typical Situation

In many organizations, there is a regularly scheduled managers'
meeting—say, it takes place at 8:30 A.M. each Monday. This becomes known as the Monday Morning Managers' Meeting. It's
held every Monday except when a holiday is celebrated on Monday, in which case the meeting is held on Tuesday morning. (We
have all seen notices saying, "The Monday morning meeting will
be held on Tuesday.")

If this is normally a one-hour meeting and you and a fellow
manager come strolling back together, some of the staff will
think or make comments like: "Well, I wonder what they decided today!" Or, "They've been gone three hours; something
big is going on." Perhaps what really happened was that the
local United Way executive had asked for a meeting to explain
some organizational changes. Since your company is an important corporate citizen, the United Way is simply building corporate support. It doesn't directly affect the company, but it's a
matter of community communication. The organization is holding a series of such informational meetings around town. The
meeting about the United Way is fairly innocuous, but if you
communicate nothing, some people are likely to assume that
something big is going on.

Everyone has a need to know what is going on. In employee
surveys, one of the higher rankings, in terms of what information is most desired, goes to "a need to know of changes that
affect me." People need to know even about things that may not
affect them; if they know nothing, they assume something.
Often that assumption is wrong, and too often it isn't even close.

As a manager or executive, you are far better off in communicating too much than communicating too little.

Let's suppose that you have thirty people in your department and you have three section supervisors who are each responsible for ten people. The three section supervisors also have some work assignments of their own. (This arrangement is typical for the first step in management.) When you return from the Monday morning meeting, call the three supervisors into your office and give them a brief overview of what went on at the meeting. They can then inform their ten staffers. You cannot allow these supervisors to "keep it to themselves." They must communicate, too.

If you follow this approach consistently, you will build a staff that will say to friends in other departments, "Our manager does a good job of letting us know what is going on." If you do otherwise, you're going to have a lot of false information floating around to correct—if you ever know about it.

18

The Human Resources Department

The human resources department (better known as HR) can be one of your biggest allies when you are beginning your management career. The department can help you out in many of the areas that new managers are not familiar with: hiring, coaching, training and development, employee assistance programs, benefits, wage and salary administration, discipline procedures, promotions, performance appraisals, dealing with difficult bosses, termination, and all the legalities involved in managing others. It is a good idea for you to familiarize yourself with what your HR department or HR person can do for you. For your own success and the success of your team, you need to build a good working relationship with HR.

A Manager's Involvement in Hiring

How much you will interact with HR depends on how much latitude you're allowed in the selection process. In many companies, HR does the initial screening of prospective employees, but the final decision is left to the appropriate manager.

The overall selection process is strengthened if the final

choice is made at the departmental or operating level. If a manager had nothing to say about the person who was hired and is unhappy with the choice, the new employee is the victim of a situation not of his or her doing. Fortunately, most companies allow the operating department to make the final selection from several qualified candidates. The usual number is from three to five qualified candidates.

Sometimes, their own bosses exclude first-time managers from the hiring process. While this exclusion may be well intentioned, it is a serious mistake. The experienced manager should, at a very minimum, include the new manager in the process. And with some seasoning, he should allow that manager to select the people for whom she will be held accountable.

Managers have a far greater commitment to the success of selections they've made than they do for those who were selected for them and then assigned. The manager should not be able to think, "I never would have hired this idiot." There will be a temptation to think in those terms when the manager has been cut out of the process.

Although people working in HR consider themselves experts on selecting employees, it doesn't matter who they think is the best qualified if the person is someone you don't want. How you react to the recommendations of HR people is important. You must take their recommendations seriously. This assumes that through talks with you they fully understand what the job requires. If they don't, it's because you haven't given them the information they need. They can't be experts on every job in the company, even with access to all the job descriptions. You're the expert on the jobs in your area of responsibility, and you ought to know what is required.

Promotion and Other Employee Matters

You'll also become involved with the HR department in promotions. Most of the time you'll try to promote employees from your own area, but when you need to look to other areas of the company for the staff you need, the people in HR will be in a position to help you. For example, they can show you the original data collected when the person was hired and most information acquired since. In most cases, they'll consult with the department that employs the person you want to promote and get important information you might not have gotten on your own.

Also, in some companies, the HR department administers employee benefit programs, so you could be going to HR on behalf of direct reports who are having difficulties with some aspect of the program.

If you haven't managed people before, HR can be a strong resource for you. You can usually go there for advice and counsel on supervisory problems you have not encountered before. The HR department is also the usual repository for books and articles on the management of people.

In many companies, the HR department handles the education and training of managers. Since this department serves the entire company, you can often talk with someone there about "people problems" that you might be reluctant to discuss with your own superior. So, you can look to HR for assistance not only in selecting people but also in managing them. The HR department can also help you with your own career development. They can suggest courses and programs you can take to improve your managerial and technical skills. They can also be consulted about promotional opportunities and develop action plans with you for how you can achieve those promotions.

Many organizations use the HR department as a place where employees can go with any problems they don't wish to discuss with their own boss. This can be a valuable service both to the employees and to the company. It is hoped that your HR department has been properly trained and educated in its function.

In short, HR will be able to assist you in your overall management job and with your personal agenda as well. To be highly regarded by HR is a great asset, so don't be a stranger in their part of the building.

19

The Current State
of Loyalty

If there is one subject that has fallen into disrepute in recent years, it is loyalty. There is a prevailing attitude that loyalty should be withheld until it is clearly proven that it is deserved: The manager shouldn't receive loyalty until he or she has earned it. The employee shouldn't receive it until it is demonstrated it has been deserved. Lastly, the company doesn't receive loyalty until everyone—management and staff—feels it is justified. So, in many organizations, the lack of loyalty means less teamwork because no one trusts or is loyal to anyone else.

Loyalty Is Out of Fashion

Unfortunately, loyalty in business is not currently in vogue. Almost everyone feels that if one company acquires another, and the announcement is made that "we plan no personnel changes in the acquired company," it is a statement with no validity. The statement itself is perceived as the first step in a major reorganization and the subsequent loss of jobs. This perception is based on many examples of wholesale layoffs just a few months after reassurances to the contrary.

There have been many greedy, ruthless acts. There also have been some reorganizations and mergers that have been a matter of survival for the companies involved. People have witnessed friends in other companies being reorganized right out of their jobs. So, there are some cynical boards, some greedy manipulators, and some concerned owners trying to save a company. At the same time, there are managers and employees who trust no one. What to do?

Showing loyalty is considered being a bit of a Pollyanna—or plain naive. In many cases that may be fair, but if loyalty gets a bad rap, then it also follows that there may be times when it is withheld and it ought to be freely given.

Do we become cynical and never show loyalty? Or do we give our loyalty until it is proved that it is not deserved? There is much to recommend the second option. Being cynical not only hurts the organization but it hurts you personally. If you have a cynical, nontrusting attitude, you become a cynic. A comedian who is a cynic can be a brilliant performer. A manager who is a cynic is a tragedy.

So, it's in your best interest to be loyal, not only to the organization but also to your manager and your employees. This means not knocking your company in the community. It means not trashing the people you supervise. Even if there are times when you feel completely justified, avoid the temptation. Disparaging remarks say more about you than they do the object of your scorn. Give the organization and its people the benefit of the doubt. It's far better to assume that your loyalty is deserved than that it's not.

20

Is There Such a Thing as Motivation?

For many managers, their definition of motivation is "to get you to do what I want you to do, with a minimum of trouble from you." That is authority, pure and simple. It is definitely not motivation. It is using your positional power to get people to do things not because they want to but because they have to.

Motivation is getting people to want to do what they are supposed to do, willingly and not by force. The best managers spend time finding out what motivates their employees, and they try to create an environment that will help their employees become self-motivated. There are many ways to find out what motivates your employees. You can observe their behavior, get to know them after a few months, or have them fill out a survey or questionnaire. There is one other method: Ask them!

Self-Motivation

The only motivation that really works is self-motivation. When you do a job because you want to, your motivation is self-perpetuating. You don't have to be bludgeoned into doing it. One of the primary responsibilities of a manager is to change the feelings of team members from "have to" to "want to."

Also, a good manager gets the job done by finding out how different people respond. If they are self-motivated, then they might be self-motivated either to get the job done or to just get by. They react in different ways, and you need to understand them well enough to know how they react and to what.

Some people are self-motivated by the possibility of a promotion. As soon as they see a relationship between their current performance and a promotion, they'll strive to perform at the top of their efficiency. Others seek their manager's approval. Since satisfactory performance is how they receive the approval, that is the route they follow. Still others like to compete in a friendly way with their peers. This type of person wants to be the best performer in the area and so will work hard at achieving that objective.

Many people are working simply for the dollar, and the way to get more dollars is to perform well to maximize the next salary increase. Many others take great personal pride in doing whatever they do well. Depending on the condition of the labor market, a number of people will be working hard to keep from being unemployed.

Some team members bring their feeling for family into their attitude toward the job, but that is often tied in turn to one of the other reasons mentioned—pursuing the dollar. They want to be able to provide more for the family, which requires more dollars.

The Manager's Role

Learning how to maximize the performance of staff is a permanent part of your daily work life. You'll have varying levels of turnover, and turnover brings in new people. You need to get to know and understand them. Your obligation in this matter deserves particular emphasis. Employees want to be understood. They want to feel important as people, not as pieces of production to get the job done. Your genuine concern for them will shine through in all you do. To understand and appreciate them doesn't mean you need be a parent figure. And you need not compromise your principles as far as quality of work is concerned.

Concern for and understanding of your staff are signs of management strength, not weakness. The so-called tough, autocratic boss may achieve satisfactory results for a while, but over the long haul, the destroyer inevitably becomes the destroyed.

Many managers believe that if you are fair, concerned, and understanding, you can't be tough when the situation demands or requires it. Nothing is further from the truth. It actually makes the show of authority much more effective because it is so rarely displayed.

There is one area, in particular, that you must handle with skill and diplomacy. Remember that some of your staff might be self-motivated because of what they can provide for their families. Of this group, some employees will respond favorably to your interest in their families, but others will consider personal inquiries an invasion of their privacy. So how does a manager handle these contradictory positions? If an employee on his own offers information about his family, you can then inquire about the family. In conversation, you'll learn about spouse, children, hobbies, and other interests. With this type of employee, you can make an inquiry such as, "How did Jeff and his team do in Little League last night?" This is a prime example of getting to know your employees, with their permission, and it fits into the concept that everyone is not motivated by the same things.

On the other hand, if you have an employee who never volunteers anything about his or her personal life, leave it alone and don't violate the obvious desire for privacy.

In getting to know your employees, there is a tendency to work with the new people and ignore the seasoned employees who do an outstanding job. Of course, it's important to bring the new people up to speed, but you must never take the outstanding employees for granted. The outstanding achievers need to know how much their quality performance is noticed and appreciated.

The Role Played by Titles

The value of titles is underestimated in far too many organizations.

Titles don't cost a company anything, so you ought to be liberal in using them as long as you maintain equity within the organization. For example, you can't have one department liberal in the use of titles and another conservative.

The banking industry is well known for this practice, and although some executives in other businesses put them down for it, I think the banks know exactly what they're doing. A customer of a bank dealing with the vice president of consumer loans will feel much more gratified than dealing with a loan clerk. The spouse of the vice president of consumer loans is surely a greater booster of the bank than the spouse of the loan clerk. In every possible way, the bank's standing in the community is elevated by this liberality with its titles.

The strange thing is that the vice president in this instance may have the same duties as the loan clerk. But which one has the more positive self-image and the stronger self-motivation? The answer is obvious.

As you move up the corporate ladder, you may have an opportunity to influence your company's policy in the use of titles. There must be an orderly manner in their use. You don't start a new employee with a super title for a routine clerical position. The title is there for the employee to aspire to reach.

A company's morale can be increased dramatically by a more enlightened use of titles. Titles can go a long way toward giving an employee a sense of well-being and of being appreciated. The next time your company has a salary freeze, consider giving a key employee a new title. You may be surprised by the positive response. She already knows she won't be getting a raise, but the new title shows that you appreciate her work and motivates her to keep doing a good job.

We all want to feel important, and so do our employees. Let's help them experience that feeling.

The Status Symbol

Another matter that falls in the motivation area is the status symbol. Obviously, status symbols work or they wouldn't find so widespread an application in the business world.

The key to the executive washroom has almost become a joke, but it is still an effective perk. The size of the office, the luxuriousness of the carpeting, wooden versus steel furniture, executive parking privileges, an executive dining room, company-paid club memberships, company-leased automobiles for executive use, corporate aircraft—the proliferation of status symbols is limited only by the expansiveness of the human imagination.

All could be considered as attempts to inspire people to raise their aspirations. These things are not important in themselves, but indicate that the employee is recognized as having arrived at a certain level in the organization. They're a lot more important to those who don't have them than to those who do. There is an old saying that goes: "Why is it that most of the people who say money isn't important are the ones who have plenty of it?" The same goes for status symbols.

A company should not become overly concerned about status symbols, but if it makes them available to its employees, it should not then criticize those same employees for longing after these methods of "keeping score." Actually, for most people, it's not the acquisition of the symbols that is important; it's what they signify to other people. Most status symbols would fall by the wayside if no one else knew you had achieved them.

It's fine for you to want to attain certain status symbols, but it's important that you keep them in proper perspective. Don't let them become so critical to you that it'll tear you up if you don't attain them as quickly as you think you should.

You cannot substitute status symbols for a satisfactory salary program or a good management approach. Unfortunately, some managers and even some companies think otherwise. They treat people badly or pay them below the competition and then figure they can make up for it with status symbols. This attitude is an insult to the intelligence of the employee. If the employee buys it, the insult is deserved.

Status symbols are the icing on the cake; they are not the cake itself. When used with intelligence and some insight into human behavior, status symbols can be a valuable tool.

Need for Achievement

Many employees have the need for achievement. Usually, they are employees whose needs of security, salary, working conditions, status, rewards, and so forth have been met. Employees who have this need usually want to be involved in decision making, want to further develop their skills and talents, find new projects and tasks challenging, and want to advance in the organization. If you can satisfy these needs, you will not only have a self-motivated employee working with you but a highly productive one as well.

Subjectivity of Motivation

Many new managers are highly motivated and that is great. But they make the mistake of believing that their employees will be motivated by what motivates them. That is not necessarily the case. Keep in mind that very different things may motivate your direct reports. That is OK. Try not to put your beliefs or value system onto others. Also remember what motivates someone today may not motivate the person next week. For example, today you may be motivated by achievement. Next week, you go out and buy a new house with a bigger mortgage. Now having job security—a steady job with a good salary—will motivate you. Try not to make assumptions about what motivates your team. You need to find out and then act upon it.

21

The Generation Gap

First-time managers can be all ages. There are new managers who are only in their twenties, many others in their thirties and forties, and some in their fifties and sixties.

Three situations exist with regard to age differences between managers and the people reporting to them:

1. The mature manager supervises people who are younger.
2. The young manager supervises people who are older.
3. The mature or young manager leads a group of varied ages, some younger, some older, and some of the same generation.

The greatest conflicts seem to occur when a young manager supervises older workers. For some reason, mature people seem to resent working for a young manager. The line most often used—and used to the point of being a cliché—is that the young manager is not "dry behind the ears." A large part of this problem is the attitude of the older employee, exacerbated by the impetuousness of youth. Therefore, we will deal primarily with the problems encountered by a young manager supervising a workforce predominately older than himself or herself.

Your approach should be nice and easy. You want the staff to think of you as mature beyond your years. If everything you do creates that impression, sooner or later it becomes a fact in everyone's mind.

Take time making changes; go slow. Don't throw your weight around by making decisions right and left, and too quickly. Many older employees will read quick decisions as being impulsive (even though they might not think the same thing if done by an older manager). Quick action by an older manager gives him the adjective "decisive." The same action by a young manager earns him the adjective "impetuous." It's not fair, but that is the way things are. What you need to do is give people time to get used to your being there. So don't build any barriers that you later need to dismantle.

Mistakes to Avoid

Often, the new manager makes changes right away, avoids the rule of incremental change, and uses all the newfound authority. That approach upsets everyone, but is especially irritable to employees who have been around a while.

You don't have to know the answer to every question brought to you. Faking an answer when you don't know it is a mistake, and the experienced employee sees through it instantly. If you can't answer a question say, "I don't know, but I'll find out and get back to you." This candor avoids the image of the know-it-all kid. In the minds of many older employees, and many not so old, you haven't lived long enough to have all the answers.

Demonstrate early on and often that, like all good managers, you are concerned about the well-being of every person reporting to you. As a manager, you need to be a salesperson. Your job is to sell your employees on the concept that they are all fortunate to have you.

Strategies for the Young Manager

Make your older employees more comfortable with your supervision by delaying some of the commonsense and fairly obvious decisions you have to make as manager. *You* know that you can make them almost immediately, but when you are new on a job, occasionally postpone your decision when it will do no damage to show your reflection on the matter.

For example, if an older employee brings you a problem that he considers serious, but about which you feel you can make an immediate decision, consider saying, "Let me think about that for a while and I'll get back to you tomorrow morning." That way you indicate that you are thoughtful and want to get all the facts, thus dispelling the young, know-it-all image. You also show that you are *not* impetuous, which is a frequent complaint about young managers.

Or, in the same situation, you might consider (with emphasis on the word *consider*) asking, "Do you have a recommendation?" or "What do you think ought to be done?" If the person bringing the problem strikes you as having common sense, give it a try. But if the person is someone who builds you a clock when you ask the time, you may be better off passing on this idea.

There is some advantage in reviewing the past performance appraisals of your direct reports when you take on a managerial job, but remember to keep an open mind. The appraisals may be generally correct, but we've all known managers with blind spots about certain staff members. We have all heard about managers who inherit an employee who supposedly never had an original idea, but by using a different approach, the manager is able to receive some good ideas from this person. So don't give up on people too soon; you may find you have the ability to reach them.

In addition, unless you already know your new, older staff members personally, consider using last names only until they suggest otherwise. Many mature employees consider younger people too familiar or presumptuous. Of course, if you are being promoted from within an office where everyone uses first names, stick to the norm. However, if you're coming in from outside, try the Mrs. Jones or Mr. Smith approach until you're fully accepted.

PART FOUR

JOB DESCRIPTIONS, PERFORMANCE APPRAISALS, AND SALARY ADMINISTRATION

22

Writing Job Descriptions

Job descriptions, performance appraisals, and salary administration are valuable functions that every company performs, either formally or informally. But if the people administering them are not properly instructed in the purpose of these functions, they can be seriously mismanaged.

We need to speak of these functions from a conceptual viewpoint. Discussion of precise details (such as the forms used) is unfeasible because of the great variety in approaches that exist between industries, and even between companies within individual industries.

Even companies without a formal program use these techniques—although often poorly. Informality is more likely to occur in smaller companies that are controlled by family members or by one or two people at the top. These individuals may feel they're being equitable and that all their employees are satisfied with the fair treatment they're receiving. That may indeed be the case, but the chances for it are remote. Even without a formal program, someone in charge decides which jobs are most important (job evaluation), makes a judgment on how well people are doing (performance appraisal), and decides how much each employee is going to be paid (salary administration). So even if the motto is "We're all like one happy family, and as papa I make all the decisions on the basis of what's fair," the company does have a program—with all the idiosyncratic biases of the "papa" thrown in.

Job Description Basics

Most companies use job descriptions, although they may range from very informal to highly structured descriptions. A job description describes *what* is done in varying detail, and it usually includes hierarchical relationships.

Some companies write their own job descriptions; others use a system designed by a management consulting service whereby some company people are trained to write the descriptions and others are taught how to score the jobs to rank them within the organization.

A job description typically tells what is done, the educational background required, how much experience is needed to perform the work competently, what the specific accountability of the job is, and the extent of supervisory or management responsibility. The description may also spell out short-term and long-term objectives and detail the relationships of people involved, including what position to which each job reports. It will often mention the personal contacts the job requires, such as with the public or governmental agencies.

The Three-Tier Approach

When writing job descriptions, you'll find it helpful to use the "three-tier approach." In this approach you specify, as mentioned previously, what the person will need to do. This is tier one: the technical skills and knowledge required.

Then you add a behavior-based tier to the description. This tier describes the way the person will need to act or behave while performing the job duties. For example, the behaviors needed in tier two might include having good follow-through, being innovative and creative, or showing a commitment to quality.

The third tier is the interpersonal skills tier. Here the requirements for a particular job might be being a good listener, being a team player, or accepting criticism from others.

Many job descriptions only focus on the technical aspects of the job, which is tier one. However, the behavioral and interpersonal ones are just as important. In fact, most experienced managers say that behavioral and interpersonal competencies are greater predictors of an individual's success on the job. When writing job descriptions make sure that each one has three tiers to it.

Job Scores

At some point, you'll write a job description, either for yourself or for some of the people reporting to you. Some companies allow the description to be written by the employee and then reviewed and corrected, if necessary, by the manager. It is best if the description is a joint effort by the employee and the manager so that there is agreement as to what the job entails. This avoids disagreements down the road.

A committee specifically trained for that purpose usually does the scoring of the job. Often, the HR department does it. We will not discuss how, because that varies by company. The points usually arrived at will determine a salary range for each job, and the range may go from new and inexperienced to a fully seasoned professional on the job. If the midpoint salary of a job is considered 100 percent, then the bottom of the range could be 75 percent or 80 percent of that and the maximum for the outstanding performance would be 120 to 125 percent of that midpoint.

Since everyone knows that the score determines salary range, the score becomes crucial in many people's minds. Therefore, there is a tendency for people to overwrite job descriptions in order to enhance the salary range. Filling a job description with such boilerplate copy usually works to a disadvantage. If a description is puffed up, it forces the committee to wade through the hyperbole to get to the facts. Job evaluation committees know exactly what the writers are doing, so the puffing up has the opposite effect. On the other hand, job descriptions that are lean and to the point aid the committee in doing its work. So, if you write a job description, avoid the temptation to load it up. The scoring committee will resent your doing it.

23

Doing Performance Appraisals

Performance appraisals can be as informal as telling someone "You've done a nice job," or as elaborate as a full-scale written report, complete with a long follow-up interview with the employee.

Clearly, all of us like to know how we're doing. One employee will say, "Working in this office is like working in the dark." Another will say, "Old Fussbudget may be tough, but you always know where you stand." It's meant as a compliment.

A formal system of performance appraisal—for example, one or two planned contacts with the employee each year for the specific purpose of discussing "how you're doing"—is preferable to the informal method, which is often equivalent to doing nothing.

Some managers are convinced that they communicate effectively with their employees and that these employees know exactly how they stand. An interview with the employees, however, will indicate that communication is one of the greatest needs they feel.

Many managers still approach their supervisory role with the motto "If I don't hear anything, I know I'm doing okay." That doesn't cut it. Top-echelon managers often avoid discussing all performances except those that require emergency action.

They feel that performance appraisals are necessary for the rank and file but members of the executive team are above such things. The rationale is that these officials are clearly in control of the situation and of themselves and don't need to be told how they're doing. Just the opposite is true. Members of the executive team often have an even greater need to be told how their superiors view their performance.

Legal Requirement

In organizations with fifty or more regular employees (this may vary by state and the nature of your business), it is a legal requirement to keep accurate and up-to-date records on every employee's performance, no matter what level he or she is. It is also a legal requirement that a formal interview take place at least once a year. The performance appraisal form is considered to be a legal document. Often in employment cases that go to court, the first thing the judge or referee will ask for is the history of performance appraisal. Performance appraisals are your organization's greatest liability when they are not done, when they are done inaccurately, and when they are done with bias.

If an employee ever tells you "I don't think so" during an appraisal meeting or after having reviewed his appraisal form or after receiving his rating, you have not done your job well. There should never be any surprises at performance appraisal time. If you have done your job of communicating constantly throughout the year and have continually told your employees how they are doing, you will never get that surprised response.

There are no specific rules for how often to review performance. Many managers have informal performance review meetings throughout the year just to ensure that there are no surprises. This is called *performance coaching*. Performance coaching is a regularly scheduled discussion between the manager and the employee to review the level of performance being met. Performance coaching is informal, can be documented if the employee wants it to be, and no forms are used. This type of coaching allows you to modify goals or set new ones, and to add or eliminate tasks or assignments.

Some companies require their managers to have quarterly sessions to avoid any surprises managers may get from their employees. A synonym for performance appraisal is *performance review*. If you think about it, this means that the once-a-year session is just a review of what has already been communicated throughout the year.

A Manager's Responsibilities

As a manager, you have a responsibility to follow some basic guidelines when writing and conducting performance appraisals. Here are the seven tenets of performance appraisal:

1. Set goals and objectives so employees know what is expected of them.
2. Provide training and coaching to help employees succeed.
3. Provide ongoing feedback on performance.
4. Prepare the paperwork for the review.
5. Conduct the review in a timely manner.
6. Understand and communicate the review's importance.
7. Be thorough and base the review on the employee's performance, not your own attitude.

The Appraisal Form

A formal system should be designed in such a way that it considers as many elements of the job as possible. The manager should be forced to make some judgment about each of the important factors. This means, first of all, that the manager must be knowledgeable about the job and the performance. That is why the appraisal should be done at the level closest to the job being reviewed. A manager three levels above the position in question can't handle the judgments as well as the manager in daily contact with the employee being appraised. It can be reviewed by higher-level management, but the appraisal will be more accurate when done by someone in daily contact with the job.

Here are some items that appear on a typical performance appraisal form. There may be anywhere from three to ten degrees of performance efficiency for each category, the extremes being "unsatisfactory" on the one end and "outstanding" on the other.

- Volumes or production levels
- Thoroughness
- Accuracy (may be identified as error rate)
- Initiative/self-starting
- Attitude
- Ability to learn
- Cooperation/ability to work with others
- Attendance and punctuality

You can probably think of other factors applying to your own business that ought to be included. Some systems may use a numeric weighting for each of the factors, arriving at a final rating that will be given to the employee. The entire form becomes a part of the employee's personnel file. The ranking scheme might be something like this:

80 to 100 points: Outstanding

60 to 80 points: Commendable

50 to 60 points: Satisfactory

40 to 50 points: Needs improvement

Less than 40 points: Unsatisfactory

The ranges can be narrower or broader if your system requires it. You'll note that in this example, 50 to 60 points generates a performance description of "satisfactory." In some companies, this would be entitled "average performance." *Satisfactory* is the better word. Most people resent being called average—they consider it demeaning. The words *satisfactory* and *needs improvement* are more useful than *average* and *below average*.

There are millions of average people in this world, but it is probably rare to find a satisfactory employee who thought he or she was just average.

Let's make another point about performance appraisals. Some managers have a rating in their mind, and they work backward to get it. You're "horsing the system" if you do that. It's usually done because the manager doesn't want to tell an employee that he needs improvement. But when you delay a tough decision, you're setting yourself up for much greater problems down the road.

Many appraisal systems have done away with terms such as *initiative, works well with others, team player,* and so forth, only to base the review and the final rating on how well the individual has met the goals set for him or her. The more objective the system is, the fairer employees feel it is.

The Interview

The interview with the employee about the performance appraisal becomes crucial. You should plan to hold it at a time when you'll be unhurried and not likely to be interrupted. Allow yourself as much time as is needed to cover all facets of the job. Answer all questions. Listen to everything the employee wants to say. Your willingness to hear your subordinate out may be as important as the discussion itself. Employees are so used to dealing with managers who behave as though everything is an emergency that, when given time to talk to their superior about their own dreams and aspirations, they may feel uncomfortable.

The conversation with your direct report is so important that you should avoid being interrupted. This should include even calls from the president of the company. The president should be informed that you are in the middle of a performance appraisal interview and let her decide if she still needs to talk to you at that time. Of course, anyone in any organization can be interrupted for emergencies, and, if that is the case, let your employee know what is happening and why you need to interrupt the appraisal meeting. It is quite disconcerting to be telling another person about your ambitions and feelings only to have the other break the spell by taking telephone calls looking at incoming e-mails.

During the performance appraisal interview, you should direct the tone of the discussion but not dominate it. You definitely have a message to convey. You want to go over each performance appraisal factor with your employee. You want to make known what you consider to be your employee's strengths on the job and what areas require some improvement. You'll seldom get disagreement on the areas you designate as strengths. But you're likely to encounter disagreement when you start discussing weaknesses. And this is where you have to allow employees to express their own feelings.

Some people will never hear anything positive if it follows something they consider negative, such as an area that "needs improvement." As a result, never start off a performance appraisal meeting with anything that might be construed by the team member as negative. Start with a couple positives.

Do you have documentation that indicates where the employee is weak and where improvement is needed? Your case is much stronger if buttressed by hard evidence. Production or quality records are much more convincing than a manager's intuition. When you come up against the team member's disagreement, that difference of opinion is important and should be discussed. It's possible that you're wrong, but you won't be if the facts can be documented.

Here is an experiment you may find helpful in getting staff to understand performance appraisals. Before sitting down to make your Solomon-like judgments, give all the members of your staff a blank form and ask them to evaluate their own performance. Then compare their appraisals with yours. You will usually find that their ratings are lower than yours. Many studies have shown that managers rate their direct reports higher than the direct reports rate themselves. The reason I suggest that you do this is because it allows you and your team members to discuss both of your views of each factor rated. You will find that your staff will learn a great deal about performance appraisal from the experiment, and you will learn a great deal more about the people you manage.

Too many leaders will be thorough in pointing out the areas in which the employee should show improvement, but they will not go far enough. If they're going to tell the employee where job performance is not up to expectations, then they must also tell *how* it can be improved. This needs to be thought through in great detail before the interview is conducted.

The Agenda

This brings us to the preparation time that is essential to a successful performance appraisal interview. You should sit down and decide what points you want to cover in the conversation. You might even prepare a brief outline of what you want to discuss. It's possible that the performance appraisal form your company uses may trigger all the proper thoughts in your mind. However, you must anticipate that it will not. You'll look foolish if you fail to cover all the bases and have to ask the employee to come back into your office a day later to review some important point that you forgot.

Make an outline of the significant items you should cover. Here are some questions you might ask as you prepare the outline:

- What areas of this employee's performance or attitude should you mention?

- What areas not covered in the performance appraisal do you need to mention?

- What are some of the items of personal interest about this employee that you should bring up?

- What questions should you ask this employee that are likely to generate some conversation and opinions about the work?

- How can you help this employee do a better job? What are the areas in which this employee will be self-motivated?

- How can you let this employee know he or she is important to you personally, not just for the work performed?

- How does this employee fit into the company's future

plans? Is this person promotable? What can you do to help?

This is the type of self-examination you should go through before beginning the session with the employee. A few minutes spent preparing for the conversation will greatly increase the success ratio of your performance appraisal interviews.

The Satisfactory Employee

Many managers prepare thoroughly for the interview with the problem employee. They know it might get sticky and they'd better see to it that their flanks are protected. You should be just as thorough in preparing for the interview with the satisfactory employee. Occasionally, you'll be surprised by the outstanding staff member who'll turn a conversation you thought was going to be all sweetness and light into a real donnybrook.

As you spend more years in management, you'll find that the satisfactory employee generally uses this interview to unload some of the problems that have been festering. The problems vary with the situation. Here are some examples:

"I'm not advancing fast enough."

"My salary is not fair for the work I do."

"My coworkers are not performing up to standards."

"As manager, you don't pay enough attention to subordinates who are getting the job done."

"Good performance is not appreciated or recognized."

You should welcome such input from your satisfactory employees, even though you risk hearing what you don't want to hear. Let's face it, many employees will tell you only what they think you want to hear; but a rare and precious few will tell the truth, and these you must listen to carefully. Don't fall into the "shoot the messenger" syndrome. Although the news a messenger brings you makes you unhappy, the fault is not with the messenger; punishing the carrier won't change the truth of the message carried. Ignorance may be bliss, but it can be fatal in a managerial career.

Of course, the information you're receiving may not exactly reflect the facts. You're receiving it through the carrier's filters. Nevertheless, that doesn't make it any less valuable. You may not have been around long enough to know how to sort out what is important and what is window dressing. If the satisfactory employee believes it's important enough to bring to your attention, then you ought to listen to it. Besides, this employee surely knows you prefer a trouble-free interview to one filled with problems, so you know the matter would not have come up unless the employee felt strongly about it.

It's possible that you may occasionally have a mischief-maker on your hands, but these people are usually not your satisfactory employees.

An Open-Door Policy

"My door is always open." How many times have you said it yourself? It doesn't take the employees long to find out what the statement really means.

"My door is always open, as long as you don't come in here to tell me about any new problems." That's one possible meaning. "My door is always open, but don't come in to talk about money or a better job." That's another. "My door is always open, but I don't want to hear about your personal problems." Your employees know what you really mean or they soon figure it out.

Then there are the managers who are likely to say, or think, "I don't want my people to like me. I just want them to respect me." Don't you find it easier to respect people you like?

Your performance appraisal interviews should encourage your employees to say whatever they have in mind. The more open the communication between both parties, the better chance that you'll have a satisfactory working relationship.

Subjectivity Factors

Even though we need to be as objective as we possibly can and treat our employees fairly, we are still human. Being human, we allow biases to creep into our evaluations of others. For example, some managers are guilty of the "halo effect." Let's say you are evaluating an employee on five different goals that she is supposed to accomplish. Let's say one of the goals is reducing the department's error rate by 5 percent. This goal means more to you than anything else. If the employee accomplishes this goal, you give her a halo, like an angel has. In your mind, the employee can do no wrong. You are blinded by the halo. When the halo effect occurs, you overrate everything else that the employee does. Halo effects occur everywhere in life. Let's use a school example. If a teacher's favorite subject is science and a child is great in science, the teacher puts a halo on that child's head and gives him a higher rating in math, science, and history because she was biased by his science aptitude.

The opposite of the halo effect is called the "horns effect." If the employee does not reduce the error rate, she gets horns over her head instead. Everything she does, even if it is great, will be diminished in the eyes of the manager because the employee has the horns.

Then there is the "recency effect." As managers—and as human beings—we tend to remember what has happened more recently. So, if employees really care about their appraisal and they know it is coming up on June 1, they will do great work during April and May. In order to avoid this effect, you need to document and keep thorough records throughout the rating period.

Another managerial subjectivity factor is the "strictness effect." Many managers believe that an employee can always improve and that no employee is perfect. Most people would all agree with that attitude. But many of those same managers would never rate anyone in the top category (for example, "exceeds expectations," or number 5). This makes no sense and can be demoralizing. If team members have exceeded their goals and performed at an incredibly high level, why not give them the top rating? These managers would probably not give the top rating even to Michael Jordan, Wayne Gretsky, or Martina Navratilova if they were employees of theirs. You've probably seen or heard of cases where a child will get a top grade, say 99 percent, on a test and a parent will ask, "What happened?" instead of praising the accomplishment. These parents obviously believe in the strictness effect. They think they are pushing their children on to greater achievement by insisting on perfection, but can you imagine what a demoralizing impact this can have on a child?

There is one more subjectivity factor or bias that can creep into performance appraisals. Many new managers or managers in general who are not familiar with their employees are guilty of "central tendency." Let's say your review system has five rating categories—1 through 5, with 5 being the highest. If a manager is not sure which category to put an employee in because he has not done his homework of setting goals, doing quarterly reviews, documenting performance, and so forth, the manager dumps the employee into the middle category. This is not fair because that employee may belong in a different rating category.

The Use of Behavioral Comments

When you write comments on the appraisal form, try to use behavioral examples that demonstrate why you rated someone as you did. For example, do not say, "James doesn't care about his work." Instead say, on January 8, February 4, and so forth, "James handed in reports after the agreed upon deadline."

Also, be very careful about the comments that you use. Remember that this is a legal document and you do not want to be open to a lawsuit. There are many documented incidents of incredibly tasteless and legally troublesome comments written by managers on appraisal forms. Make sure you never write a comment like any of the following examples:

- "The wheel is turning but the hamster is dead."
- "One neuron short of a synapse."
- "The gates are down, the lights are working, but the train is nowhere to be found."
- She has a full six-pack, but she does not have that plastic thing to hold it all together."
- "Bright as Alaska in December."

Post Appraisal

When you have completed the appraisal interview, it is a good idea to review how you did so you can improve and do better on the next interview. Here is a checklist that will help you out. Ask yourself if you:

- Explained the purpose of the interview?
- Found out the employee's views and feelings on his performance?
- Allowed the employee to do the majority of the talking?
- Pointed out where the employee is doing well?
- Offered suggestions for improving performance and asked the employee for suggestions (if necessary)?
- Put the employee at ease by creating a relaxed environment?
- Agreed on action plans for improving performance (if necessary)?
- Set a time frame for improving performance (if necessary)?

Closing Thought

Performance appraisals are hard work. You need to keep accurate documentation, communicate constantly throughout the year, follow legal guidelines, fill out the forms correctly, conduct an effective interview, and then examine how the entire process went. The appraisal process is also quite time consuming. But if you do a great job here, you will have employees who know what is expected of them because they have your assurance that you will be working with them to help them succeed. Performance appraisals—if they are done well, taken seriously by you, and are fair—can be a great motivator for each of your employees.

24

Salary Administration

It should be obvious that job descriptions, performance appraisals, and salary administration all fit together in one overall plan. They are designed to provide accurate descriptions of what people do, give fair evaluations of their performance, and pay them a salary that is reasonable for their efforts. All these factors must bear a proper relationship to one another and make a contribution to the organization's overall goals.

If you have a job evaluation program, you probably also have salary ranges for each position in the organization. As a manager, you work within that scale.

It makes sense to have a minimum and a maximum salary for each position. You can't allow a situation to develop in which an individual could stay on the same job for years and receive a salary out of all proportion to what the task is worth. It's important to make certain that long-term employees are aware of this situation, especially as they get close to the salary "lid" on the job. For most well-qualified people this is not a problem, because they'll usually be promoted to another job with a larger salary range. However, in your managerial career, you will encounter long-term employees who remain in the same jobs. Perhaps they don't want to be promoted. Perhaps they are at their level of competence and cannot handle the next position up the ladder.

These people need to know that there is a limit to what the job is worth to the organization. You have to tell these individuals that once they are at the maximum, the only way they can receive more money is if the salary ranges are changed on all jobs. This may happen, for example, through a cost-of-living increase that raises the ranges on all jobs by a certain percent. Should that occur, you would have a little room for awarding salary increases.

Nonetheless, long-term employees who stay in the same job for an extended period of time and who are at maximum salary level need to have continued incentive. They are capable and should be kept on the job. Many companies have solved this problem by instituting annual financial awards (such as annual, increasing cash stipends) related to years of service. This keeps financial payments out of the job evaluation system and yet rewards the faithful long-term employee.

The salary administration program for all other employees usually includes a salary recommendation within a range of pay increases, based on the kind of performance appraisal the employee has received. Since the two procedures have such an impact on each other, some companies separate the salary recommendation from the performance appraisal rating. In that way, a manager's idea of what a salary increase ought to be is not allowed to determine the performance appraisal given. If as manager you make both determinations at the same time, you'll be tempted to take the answer you want and work backward to justify it. It remains difficult to separate salary consideration from the performance appraisal, but completing the procedures several weeks or months apart may help.

So let's assume your company does have salary ranges for each job and there is some limitation on what you can recommend. No doubt the salary ranges overlap. For example, a veteran employee on a lower-level job could be paid more than a newer employee on a higher-level job. An outstanding performer at one level could be paid more than a mediocre worker one level up.

Equity

As the manager, you're concerned with equity. You should review the salaries of all the people who report to you. You might begin by listing all the jobs in your department, from top to bottom. You might then write the monthly salary next to each name. Based on what you know about the job performances, do the salaries look reasonable? Is there any salary that looks out of line?

Another method you can use is to rank the jobs in the order of importance to the department, as you perceive the situation. How does that compare with top management's evaluation of the importance of the jobs? If there are differences you can't reconcile or accept, then you'd better schedule a session with your immediate superior to see what can be done about it.

In this matter of rankings, appraisals, and salaries, a word of caution is in order. This is an extremely important point. Recognize—and be willing to admit to yourself—that you like some employees more than others. You're conning yourself if you think you like them all equally. Certain personality types are more agreeable to you than others. Try as honestly as you can to keep these personality preferences from unduly influencing the decisions you make about appraisals, salaries, and promotions.

In recommending a salary increase for several employees, you'll have some tricky decisions to make. If the company makes all its salary adjustments at the same time each year, then it's fairly easy to compare one recommendation against another. You can make all your decisions at one time and see how they stack up with one another. But if salary decisions occur throughout the year—for example, if they are tied to the worker's employment anniversary—it's more difficult to have all the decisions spread out in front of you.

Although maintaining equity in this type of situation is difficult, it is possible if you keep adequate records. Retain copies of all your job descriptions, performance appraisals, and salary recommendations. Some companies encourage supervisors not to keep such records and to depend on the personnel department's records. However, maintaining your own set is worth the effort; you'll then have the records when you want them. Keep these records in a file that is locked, and do not allow any employee access to the file, including the secretary or assistant who works closely with you.

The Salary Recommendation

In making a salary recommendation, be as sure as you possibly can that it's a reasonable amount. It should be neither too low nor too high and at the same time fit within the framework of the performance the company is receiving from that person. An increase that is too high, for example, could create an "encore" problem. Anything less than the same amount offered the next time around may be considered an insult by the employee. However, an unusually large increase coming at the time of a promotion doesn't run that same encore danger because it can be tied to a specific, nonrepeating situation. In that case, you must explain to the employee why the increase is so large and why it doesn't create a precedent for future increases.

Since a small increase can be considered an insult, you'd perhaps do better to recommend no increase at all rather than a pittance. Sometimes a small increase is a cop-out, and is given because the supervisor lacks the courage to recommend no increase. But this only postpones the inevitable reckoning; you are better off confronting the situation immediately and honestly.

When considering the amount of the raise, it's essential that you not allow the employee's need to be an important factor. This may seem inhumane, but consider these points. If you based salary increases on need, the employee in the most desperate state of need would be the highest paid. If that person were also the best performer, you'd have no problem. But what if the employee's performance was merely average?

The common thread that must run through salary administration is merit. Basing your salary recommendations on who has been with the company the longest, who has the greatest number of children, or whose mother is ill moves you away from your responsibilities as a salary administrator and puts you in the charity business. If you have direct reports with financial problems, you can be helpful as a friend, a good listener, or a source of information about where to go for professional assistance, but you can't use the salary dollars you're charged with as a method of solving the social problems of your direct reports.

When you're making a salary adjustment for an employee who's having difficulty, there is a great temptation to add a few more dollars than you would otherwise. You must resist that temptation and base your decision strictly on the performance of the individual employee.

PART FIVE

IMPROVING AND

DEVELOPING YOURSELF

25

Having Emotional Intelligence

There is a relatively new management concept called *emotional intelligence* that is causing quite a stir. Social scientists and psychologists are finding that managers and leaders who have high levels of emotional intelligence, or a high emotional quotient (EQ), seem to do much better in their managerial and leadership roles than their counterparts who have average or low EQs. These experts have also found that individuals high in EQ experience more career success, build stronger personal relationships, enjoy better health due to better stress management techniques, motivate themselves and others to achieve greater accomplishments, and have the capacity to trust others and be trusted. According to these same experts, traditional IQ seems to have no bearing on managerial success.

History of EQ

The concept of emotional intelligence was made popular in the 1995 book *Emotional Intelligence: Why It Can Matter More Than IQ*, written by Dr. Daniel Goleman. Since the book's publication, there have been many articles and books written on the topic. In addition, practically every well-respected management-training program now has a module or two on how to be emotionally intelligent.

IQ

IQ, or intellectual quotient, comprises competencies quite different from those of EQ. People high in IQ have great mathematical abilities. They also have extensive understanding of vocabulary and language, test high in abstract reasoning and spatial abilities, and have excellent comprehension skills. For the most part, IQ level is determined at birth. That is, there is a large genetic predisposition to how high one's IQ will be. Over the years, IQ scores can change, but probably not more than fifteen points on the average. On the other hand, emotional intelligence is a learned behavior. An EQ score can change dramatically over the years.

EQ

Having emotional intelligence basically means that you have emotional smarts. If you can answer yes to the following questions, you probably have high levels of emotional intelligence.

- Can you walk into a room and sense the mood?
- Can you recognize the emotional states of others?
- Do you know when you are becoming emotional and can you control it if you wanted to?
- Under stressful and chaotic situations, can you evoke positive emotions in others?
- Can you and do you express to others how you are feeling and what your emotions are?

These EQ abilities seem to be very close to the supportive behaviors we mentioned earlier. EQ is a combination of having people skills and knowing a lot about yourself.

The EQ Test

Let's have a little fun now. Below are ten items that determine EQ levels. For each item, rate your own ability on a scale of 1 to 10, with 10 being the highest. Be honest if you want to get an accurate score.

1. When in stressful situations, I find ways to relax. _____
2. I can stay calm when others verbally attack me. _____
3. I can easily identify my own mood shifts. _____
4. It is easy to "come back" after a major setback. _____
5. I have effective interpersonal skills like listening, giving feedback, and motivating others. _____
6. It is easy for me to show empathy to others. _____
7. I know when others are distressed or upset. _____
8. Even when working on a boring project, I can show high levels of energy. _____
9. I just seem to know what others are thinking. _____
10. I use positive, instead of negative "self-talk." _____

A score above 85 means you are already emotionally intelligent. A score above 75 means you are well on your way to becoming emotionally intelligent.

EQ and Managing

No doubt you can see the connection between EQ and being a successful manager. Managing people is very different from managing tasks and projects. Having the EQ skills of recognizing your own feelings and the feeling of others, being able to express your emotions appropriately, being self-motivated and getting others to be, and being able to deal with stress, tension, and chaos and helping others do the same, mark the excellent manager of today's workplace.

26

Developing a Positive Self-Image

Having a realistic opinion of your own ability is not an ego problem if it's a realistic assessment of your situation.

People can get awfully mixed up in dealing with this ego thing. There are always people around who want you to feel guilty if you have a healthy opinion of yourself. Rather, it is "love your neighbor as yourself." This implies that your capacity to love your neighbor is determined by your capacity to love yourself. This principle applies to management, too.

Many excellent books have been written on the subject of self-image, and they have important concepts in them for the manager. Here are a few basics that will help you in your managerial career.

The fact is, we fall or rise by our self-image. If we have a low opinion of ourselves and believe we're going to fail, our subconscious will try to deliver that result to us. Conversely, if we have a high opinion of ourselves and think we're going to succeed, our chances for success are greatly increased. That is an oversimplification, but it conveys the thought. If you think success, if you look successful, if you're confident of being successful, you greatly increase your chances to be successful. It's primarily a matter of attitude. If you believe that you are a failure, that is what you're likely to be.

Closely related to this is the management concept called the *self-fulfilling prophecy*. Basically, the prophecy states that we treat people the way we are told they behave or the way we think they will behave. Much research has been done with managers and the self-fulfilling prophecy. Here is an example of one research study:

Two managers, both considered to be excellent, were told that they each would be leading a new project team. One manager (X) was told he had the best employees in the company. The other manager (Y) was told he had "average" employees. In reality, they both had average employees. Separately, they were given all the details of their project. Unknown to them, both managers had the exact same instructions and were working on the same project. After two weeks, which manager do you think had better results at the completion of the project? Right. It was manager X. He believed he had the best employees. Thus he pushed them more, delegated more to them, and expected much more from them. Be careful that you do not fall prey to the self-fulfilling prophecy either about others or yourself.

To reinforce a successful attitude, you need some success along the way. Now that you've moved into your first managerial position, every success you have will serve as a building block to further achievements.

It should be obvious that you can't substitute feelings of success for actual accomplishments. You can't have the appearance without any substance. That would be a sham. You'll soon be found out, and to your own disadvantage.

An Impression of Arrogance

One of the most serious problems observed in newly appointed young managers is the impression they give of arrogance. Be careful that you don't mishandle your feelings of success so that you are misconstrued as being arrogant. A manager can feel pride in having been elevated into the managerial ranks without appearing cocky. Rather, the impression conveyed should be one of quiet confidence.

Do you suspect that there are people in your organization who don't believe you were the right selection and who'd delight in your failure? That is not only possible; it's quite likely. An appearance that can be construed as arrogance is going to convince these people that they're correct in their assessment of you.

Strategies for Improving Self-Image

Anyone can work on improving his or her self-image. Here are three methods that have proven successful. The first method is called *visualization*. You try to visualize doing something that is important to you. It may be closing a big contract, getting a round of applause for conducting a seminar, or getting that smile of affection from a loved one for showing support. You may want to visualize getting your point across with your CEO, or disciplining an employee, or doing a presentation in front of the board of directors. What happens in visualization, after periods of practice, is that these visual images become part of how we view our actions and ourselves. The brain literally records these visual pictures for later use.

The next method is called *win-win*. In this method, you give people a lot of positive feedback and work hard to help others succeed. This makes you feel better about their work as well as your abilities as a manager.

The last technique is *positive self-talk*. It is estimated that we send ourselves more than 1,000 messages a day. If you want to build up your self-image, make sure that these messages are positive ones. The more you do this, the more the brain builds a positive sense of self. Examples of positive self-talk include the following:

- "I am improving my management skills each day."
- "I can handle this."
- "I made a mistake but I will do better next time."

Positive self-talk is like having a CD playing in your mind that sends you only positive messages.

Skittish About Mistakes

In carrying out your duties as a manager, you'll make an occasional mistake. You'll exercise bad judgment. It happens to all of us. How you view and handle these mistakes is important not only to your own development, but also in how others perceive you. Be completely honest with yourself and everyone you associate with. Don't try to cover up a mistake, rationalize it, or—worse—imply that it might be someone else's fault. Many managers have trouble getting the following two statements out of their mouths: "I made a mistake" and "I'm sorry." It's as though the words are stuck in their throats and can't be expelled. These statements are not signs of weakness. They are signs of confidence in your humanity.

New managers have difficulty accepting responsibility for the mistakes of people who report to them. So skittish are these managers about mistakes that they avoid criticism by handling the more complex work themselves. When they do this, they shut off their promotion possibilities, and kill themselves with overwork, which is a grim prospect.

The way to solve this problem is to build your entire managerial role. You become and select better trainers; you become a better selector of people; you develop better internal controls that minimize the mistakes and their impact. And when mistakes happen and you're the culprit, you admit it, correct it, learn from it, and—above all—don't agonize over it. Then you and the staff move on.

Self-Infatuation and Self-Contradiction

You have to put forth your best image, but don't be so successful at it that, like the movie star, you fall for your own publicity. Be willing to admit to yourself what your shortcomings are. You'd be surprised at how many managers can't do that. They, of course, have shortcomings. They can't be experts at everything. But in ascending to their exalted position, they find that everyone starts catering to them. It takes an unusual manager to realize that all that honorific treatment doesn't increase intelligence or boost knowledge. It's easy and pleasant to sit back and accept all that bowing and scraping. The manager is soon convinced that the adoration is deserved. Perhaps the charisma you think is personal is merely created by the position you hold.

The *infallibility syndrome* becomes most noticeable at the level of chief executive officer. Between the beginning manager and the top post are varying degrees of infallibility that seem to go with the job. You have to keep an honest perspective on who you are. If tomorrow you were named CEO, you wouldn't automatically become smarter than you were yesterday. But people would start listening to you as though you were one of the Three Wise Men. You didn't get smarter; you just gained more power. Don't confuse the two!

Pay little attention to what executives say in this regard. Pay more attention to what they do. If an executive says, "I hire people who are smarter than I am," think about what he does. Do all the people he hires seem to be clones of him? If an executive says, "I encourage my people to disagree with me. I don't want to be surrounded by yes men," remember what happened last week when the executive snapped off the head of a subordinate who did express a different point of view. If an executive says, "My door is always open," and then looks visibly upset when you walk in saying, "Do you have a moment?" the words ring hollow, indeed. The words are contradicted by actions and attitude.

Throughout your business life, you'll encounter executives who espouse beautiful management philosophies. The main problem is that they wield their authority using other, less desirable concepts. So be honest with yourself, recognize who you are and try to get your performance to reflect your philosophy.

Shortcomings and Prejudicial Mind-Sets

Do not advertise your weaknesses. That's foolish, but be willing to admit them to yourself and do all you can to correct them. For example, the things that you probably don't do well are also the things that you don't enjoy. That's hardly a coincidence. But you'll get through those chores you don't like if you exercise some self-discipline and get them out of the way. Remember that, in your performance appraisal, the quality of your work will not excuse errors in the tasks you don't like. So, even the tasks you don't care for demand quality performance. Every job has aspects to it that you're not going to like; get them done well, so they are out of the way and you can get to the parts that are fun.

Be willing to admit mind-sets or attitudes of yours that may be a problem. You can't take the edge off them if you can't admit them. For example, think of the manager who has a prejudice against other managers who leave the office at five. He believes that when people become managers, their work comes first and social and family obligations have to wait. He also believes that any manager who leaves so early could not possibly have gotten all their work done or done it well. That's his prejudice; it's his mind-set. It's not provable; it's an emotional feeling he has. In dealing with managers who have a life outside of work, this type of manager must be aware of his mind-set and make every effort to overcome it—but without overcompensating for it. It's a tough situation, but we must first be willing to admit a fault before we can deal with it.

Your Objectivity

Through the years we have all come across a great number of managers who tell you they're looking at a problem objectively, and then proceed to explain their attitudes or solutions in a most subjective way. When a manager starts off by claiming to be completely objective, you must wonder why the statement is being made. Does he or she protest too much? This preamble is a giveaway.

It's unlikely that you will ever be able to be completely objective. We are the sum of all our experiences. We like some of our staff better than others, and you may not even be able to explain why. It could be personal chemistry. As long as you recognize that, you can compensate by dealing fairly with those who are less liked.

It seems better for the manager to not even bring up the

subject of objectivity or subjectivity. How about being as honest as you can be in your dealings with people, and not get into all the shadings of objectivity and subjectivity? The recognition of how difficult it is to be completely objective is a great place to begin.

When your manager asks you, "Are you being objective?" your answer ought to be, "I try to be." No one can guarantee that he or she is completely objective, but the effort in that direction is laudatory.

Quiet Confidence

Develop quiet confidence in your decision-making ability. As you make more and more decisions, you will get better at it. Most management decisions do not require Solomon-like wisdom; they require the ability to develop the facts and know when you have enough information to make the decision.

Don't make emotional decisions and rationalize them afterward. When you do, you will find yourself defending a decision that you wish you hadn't made. A bad decision is not worth defending, even if you're the person who made it. Once you rationalize a bad decision, you're trapped.

Too many new managers believe that they have to be fast decision makers in order to be successful. This creates an image of shooting from the hip, which is not a desirable image to foster. The other extreme is not getting your gun out of the holster. Balance and moderation are the keys. You don't want your staff saying, "She makes decisions too quickly," nor do you want them to say, "She has trouble making decisions." If your employees and your own manager were to rank your decision-making style, what you're after is "just right."

Decision-Making Modes

It is also important for your confidence to be able to use a variety of decision-making modes. Sometimes you will have to make the decision yourself. You do this when you are the expert or time is short. Other times, you will need to get the input from your staff and have them help you make the decision. And there could be other times when you would allow the team to make the decision for you. You would use this decision-making mode when the team is more knowledgeable than you are. Don't be the type of manager who uses only one method of making decisions. Be flexible in your approach. When you are able to select the correct decision mode for the situation, your confidence and self-image will soar.

Promotion and Self-Promotion

As we already mentioned, you're judged by the performance of your area of responsibility. The people who report to you are as important to your future as are the people to whom you report. That leads directly to the matter of office politics. It exists everywhere. People recoil at the idea of office politics, and that is because all people do not hold politics and politicians in high regard. One of the meanings of *politics,* which certainly has a positive spin, is "the total complex of relations between people in society." The game of office politics exists, and nearly everyone plays it. You're either a player or a spectator. Most managers are players.

Office Politics: Playing the Game

Some people are viewed as "cold turkeys" by those who report to them but as "warm, generous human beings" by their superiors. These people are really playing the game, but in the long run they're sure to fail. However much they may succeed in fulfilling their ambitions at the office, they'll fail as human beings.

If getting promoted is more important to you than your integrity, than being your own person, then you better skip the rest of this chapter because you won't like much of what is said in it.

Almost anyone can succeed temporarily by being an opportunist, but consider the price that is been paid in getting there.

Granted, many of the decisions made about promotions will not seem fair to you, and they won't all be made on the basis of ability. No one guaranteed you that life would be fair, so don't expect it.

Often, individuals feel that most promotions are made on the basis of something other than fairness and ability. But even though most companies try to make these decisions fairly, it doesn't always come off that way. Besides, a decision that seems perfectly rational to the executive who is making it may not seem rational to you, especially if you thought you were the likely candidate for the promotion.

In spite of that, you still have to prepare yourself for it to get promoted. If you depend on luck or serendipity, your chances are greatly diminished. You have everything to gain and nothing to lose by being prepared. Who knows, your opportunity for promotion may come from outside your company. You want to be prepared for that possibility, too.

Preparing Your Understudy

As soon as you've mastered your job, you must start looking for an understudy. The reason for this is clear. If the company refuses to consider candidates to replace you, it may view you as indispensable in your current position and you may be passed up for promotion.

Finding the appropriate understudy can be a delicate matter. You should not select your crown prince or princess too early. If the candidate doesn't develop properly and fails to demonstrate the skills needed to move into your job, you could have a serious problem. Changing your mind about a successor you've already selected is like opening a can of worms.

How you go about preparing for your own replacement is of critical importance. If you already have an assistant who is perfectly capable in the job, it's merely a matter of helping that assistant to develop as thoroughly and as rapidly as possible.

Give your assistant bits and pieces of your job to perform. Under no circumstance should you delegate your entire job to your assistant and then sit back and read newspapers and business magazines. The company obviously didn't put you in the position for that purpose.

Allow your assistant to do more and more aspects of your job until most of it has been learned. Make sure the assistant does each section of the job frequently enough that it won't be forgotten. Occasionally, invite the assistant to participate in the interviewing process when you're hiring new employees.

Assuming the assistant is performing satisfactorily, start your political campaign for your prospective replacement. Make sure your boss knows how well the person is developing. On performance appraisals, use terms and phrases such as "promotable" and "is developing into an outstanding management prospect." Of course, never say these things if they're untrue; that would probably work to the disadvantage of both you and your assistant. But if the assistant is developing well, communicate it up to the next level without being blatant about it.

You run the risk that the assistant might get promoted out from under you. It's still a risk worth taking. Even if this happens to you several times, you'll get the reputation of being an outstanding developer of people. That will add to your own promotability. Besides, you'll find that developing employees can be a highly satisfying experience. And while you're worrying about preparing your people for promotion, it's hoped that your own boss is just as concerned about you and your future.

Using Multiple Choices

If you don't have an assistant already in place, you should assign parts of your job to several people and see how they run with the added responsibility and the new opportunity. This is indeed to your advantage, since training several replacements at once makes it unlikely that all the candidates will be promoted out from under you. This in-depth backstopping will serve you well in emergencies.

Don't be in too big a hurry to move a single candidate into the position of assistant. The moment you name a person as your assistant, others stop striving for the job. That is the trouble with any promotion. Those who don't get it stop aspiring to it, which usually has an adverse effect on their performance, even though it may be temporary.

The following management concept may be of value to you: Always hold something out for your team members to aspire to. If you get to the point where you have to select a single team member as your heir apparent, then let the other candidates know that opportunities still exist for them in other departments, and that you'll help them toward their goal of a promotion.

But as long as you continue to have several prospects vying for the position, you must treat them as equals. Rotate the assignments among them. Make sure that all of them are exposed to all aspects of your job. If you're gone from the office occasionally, put each in charge of the operation in turn. Give them all a chance at managing the personnel aspects of the job, too.

On some regular basis, meet with all the candidates at once and discuss your job with them. Don't say, "Let's discuss my job." Rather, talk about some specific problems they've encountered. All of them will benefit from the discussion. If one of them had to face an unusual management problem in your absence, why shouldn't all of them profit from the experience?

Avoiding the Perils of Indispensability

Once again, it is important to not allow yourself to become indispensable. Some managers trap themselves into this kind of situation. In their effort to ensure the quality of the work, they request that all difficult questions be referred to them. It doesn't take long for employees to figure out that anything out of the ordinary will soon be going to you as the boss. It isn't the time taken from your day that creates problems. The more fundamental trouble is that your people soon stop trying to work out the more complex problems by themselves.

It's important that your people be encouraged to find answers on their own. They'll be better employees for it. There are limits, of course, to the areas of responsibility that can be delegated to them, but you're better off erring on the side of too much latitude in delegating responsibility than too little. It's good management to allow staff members some responsibility while still assuring them that the executive is accountable for their performance.

You've heard people worrying about whether the company would get along without them while they're on vacation. They have it backward: Their real worry is that the company *will* get along just fine without them. The manager who is doing the right kind of job in developing employees and backup management can leave with the assurance that the department will function smoothly in his or her absence. The truly efficient and dedicated executive, indeed, has progressed to the point where he or she can even be gone permanently—to a promotion in another company. There are managers who, in a misguided view of what their job required, made themselves indispensable and spent the rest of their business careers proving it—by never being moved from that position.

The main problem with such people is that they don't understand what the job of management is about. Management isn't doing—it's seeing that it gets done.

Following Your Predecessor

It helps a great deal if your predecessor in the job was a real dunderhead, who left the place in a shambles. Unless you're a complete loser, you'll look like a champion by comparison. That is preferable to stepping into a smooth-running operation. Following a company hero who is retiring or left to take a much higher level position at another organization is difficult because, no matter how well you perform, it's tough to be compared with a hero and the legend that time bestows upon him.

So if you ever have a choice between moving into an area of chaos or assuming a nice, clean operation, go with the disaster. It could be a great opportunity to establish a reputation that will stay with you your entire career. You'll not regret it.

Continuing Your Education

In preparing yourself for promotion, consider extending your knowledge of the business you're in. It's not enough to become expert in your restricted area of responsibility. You must understand more about your company's entire operation.

You can acquire this additional knowledge in several ways. For instance, you can broaden your knowledge through selected readings. Your own boss may be able to recommend published material that fits closely into your own company's operation and philosophy. No boss is ever insulted when asked for advice. However, a word of caution: Don't ask for advice too often, because your boss will either suspect you can't make up your own mind about too many things or figure you're seeking a favor. Neither of these reactions will help your cause.

If your company offers education programs, sign up for them. Even if you can't see any immediate benefit from them, they'll serve you well over the long haul. In addition, you're displaying an eagerness to learn.

Dressing for Success

Styles come and go, so what is inappropriate for business today may seem satisfactory in a couple of years, or even months, down the road. As a manager, you should not try to be a trendsetter by wearing far-out, extreme, avant-garde clothing. You might not think it fair, but you will not advance your career if some executive refers to you, in conversations, as "that kooky dresser down on the first floor."

What is acceptable or extreme may vary by the kind of business you are in or the area of the country. For instance, what might work in a fashion magazine's office would seem inappropriate in a tradition-bound life insurance company. What may be acceptable in the southwestern part of the country may not sit well in the East. Obviously, what you wear as a manager in a factory is altogether different from what you wear in an office. The point is that if you are going to be successful, it helps if you look successful—but not extreme. You should make a quiet statement, not a loud clatter.

The following story points out how dress can differ from company to company. Several years ago, a young man had an interview scheduled at one of the more creative departments within a motion picture studio in Hollywood. He called up his contact there and asked her what the dress was. She replied, "casual." So, the young man arrived in slacks and a nice pressed shirt. He walked into the room and everyone was dressed in tank tops and shorts! The word *casual* obviously meant different things to the interviewee and to his contact. Despite being on a different wavelength, however, the young man still landed the job.

This story proves more than that companies have different ideas on style and dress. It shows that you'll make fewer fashion mistakes as a businessperson by being a bit overdressed than by being underdressed. If you go to an event wearing a suit and tie, and you find it's casual when you arrive, you can always take off the jacket and tie. If you go casually and find that everyone is in a suit and tie, you cannot easily add the apparel to get in compliance.

A rule of thumb is this: If you're not sure what to wear, you're better off erring on the side of overdressing.

Tooting Your Own Horn, but Softly

You can be the greatest thing since sliced bread, but if you're the only one who knows it, you won't go anywhere with your many talents. You need to get the word to the people you report to, in the most effective way possible.

If you're obviously tooting your own horn, people are going to react negatively. You may come off as a blowhard—a reputation you do not need. There are people with a great deal of ability who are too blatant in their self-promotion. It turns people off and has the opposite effect of the intended result.

You must be subtle. You want the reaction of effectively communicating.

The following example shows how a situation might be handled so as not to be offensive to others and not generate a negative reaction: Let's say the local community college is offering courses that you think might help you do your job better, and thereby make you more promotable. Here are some ways to make sure your boss and the company are aware of your educational efforts. (Anything that gets the job done without overkill is after the goal.)

- Send a note to the human resources department, with a copy to your boss, asking that your personnel records show that you're taking the course. That puts the information in your file, where anyone examining your record and looking at candidates for promotion will see it. Upon completing the course, again notify HR, this time of the successful conclusion.

- Engage in casual conversation with your boss (if he or she hasn't acknowledged the copy of the note to HR), and mention something along the lines of "one of the students in my accounting class said something funny last night. . . ." The boss may ask, "What accounting class?"

- Place the textbooks on your desk. Eventually the desired question may be asked.

- Ask your boss for clarification of a class discussion item that you did not fully understand.

- If you have a classmate to the office for lunch, introduce her to your boss. "Mr. Jones, I'd like you to meet my accounting classmate, Nelda Smith."

You get the idea. The subtler you are, the less likely it is that your efforts will come off as braggadocio. Your boss, who knows something about self-promotion, recognizes that you are communicating about your accomplishments. If you do it well, he or she may even admire your style.

With an apology to the Bible, "What profit it a man if he becometh the most qualified new manager in the company if no one knoweth it?" Too few bosses will approach you and say, "Tell me—what are you doing to prepare yourself for promotion?" So you have to help them.

Some executives espouse the philosophy that if you do a great job, the promotions and raises will take care of themselves. This is a risky strategy, and you can't afford to take such chances. If your superiors don't know what you're doing, how can your accomplishments be taken into consideration? Develop a style of communicating the important aspects of your development, but do it with a degree of understatement so that others are not offended or construe you as too pushy.

But Is the Game Worth the Candle?

Being an outstanding manager and concurrently working up to the next rung on the ladder is a constant in almost every manager's career—unless you lose interest in moving higher. There is nothing wrong with not wanting to pay the price of moving to the next level. That is healthy if it's what you feel, because it means you're in touch with yourself. We all may reach a point where we are no longer considered promotable. Also, we may still be considered promotable, but we are comfortable where we are and don't want the aggravation that goes with the next promotion. Besides, the promotion pyramid gets much narrower the closer it gets to the top. Even the chairperson and CEO are no longer promotable—at least in the present company.

In earlier editions of this book, it was mentioned that you have a right to know where you stand, as far as promotability is concerned. It was even suggested that there was nothing wrong with *pressing* for that information. Let's rethink this. If you don't care to be promoted, why ask? If you're offered a promotion, that's flattering and you might even change your mind.

If you want to be promoted, and you think a promotion is long overdue, why ask and have some boss say, "No, I don't believe you are promotable," or have your boss dodge the question and leave you unsatisfied? If you ask, and your boss puts a note in your file like, "Manager Jones pressed me about promotion. Told him, 'He's topped out.'" Now, let's say your boss leaves and goes to another company, and you're getting along famously with the new executive. You'd rather not have that "he's topped out" comment in your file. Why trigger that possible response—which may be faulty—and have it carved in stone?

If you are desirous of additional promotions, it helps to keep your eye on the ball and not be distracted by some future possibility. The greatest favor you can do to your career is to be outstanding at the job you hold right now. Mastering your current job is your first priority. Every other ambition must be secondary to that objective.

Acquiring a Sponsor

It helps to have a boss who sings your praises at the executive level. Develop good relationships with all the executives with whom you come in contact, who know the quality of your performance, and who recognize your healthy upbeat attitude. If the only one who thinks highly of you is your boss, and he or she leaves the company for some super job in another organization, you've lost your advocate—unless your boss offers you a great job in his or her new company. It helps if many executives in the organization know your name in positive terms. Being sponsored by several star executives is a great thing. Gladly accept any committee assignment that puts you in contact with managers and executives beyond your own department.

Having Style and Merit

Achieving the objectives discussed in this chapter requires excellent performance on your part and confidence in yourself. Often, the difference between a satisfactory job and a great job is image or style. Your style colors a superior's perception of your performance, especially if the style is one to which your superior reacts positively. But a bad or offensive style is similarly critical in evoking a negative response.

Doing a great job and maximizing the mileage you get out of that is one thing; conning people into thinking you're doing an outstanding job when you're not cutting the mustard is quite another and will create problems. The message and the performance must be synchronized.

27

Managing Your Own Time

Have you ever come home from the office with the feeling that you didn't accomplish any of the things you wanted to get done that day? We all have days like that, spent entirely in putting out brushfires. Sometimes it can't be helped, but if it's happening to you regularly, part of the problem may be your own lack of time management.

Smaller Segments

The following approach to time management has worked wonders for a successful nonfiction author. Let's hear it in his own words:

> "When I first started writing seriously about ten years ago, I'd set a goal of writing a full chapter every week, yet the entire week would go by without my having written a single line. The reason was my perception of needing to block out many hours for a chapter. Nothing was happening. Then I decided to break my goal down into smaller segments. The goal became to write two pages each day. Occasionally, I'd miss a day; then I'd set a goal of four pages for the next day. If for some unforeseen reason I missed

167

more than two days, I did not make the goal a cumulative one, or I'd be right back to the block I had with the entire chapter.

"As a result of setting more reasonable goals, I started getting material written, even though other demands on my time remained unchanged. The only change was my attitude toward, and approach to, the problem. Sometimes I would sit down to write my two pages and ended up writing much more, ten or fifteen. If I had established a goal for that day of fifteen pages, I would not have begun to write, owing to the lateness of the hour."

The List

You've probably heard of the late U.S. industrialist Henry Kaiser. Among his many achievements was establishing a company that built cargo vessels called Liberty ships during World War II. These ships were fully constructed in a matter of days, truly a spectacular accomplishment.

The first thing Kaiser did on entering the office in the morning was to sit at his desk with a legal-size pad on which he listed the items he wished to accomplish that day and put the items on the list in priority order. During the day, the list remained on top of the desk. As a goal was accomplished, a line was drawn through it on the pad. Goals that didn't get accomplished that day would be put on the next day's list. Kaiser always tried to work on his priority items first.

Try this simple approach to organizing your day and you will be pleasantly surprised at how much more you are able to accomplish. You're forced to plan the day's activities as you write the day's objectives on the pad. That's probably the greatest value of the technique.

There is one modification you might make in this system, however, that may make it even more useful. You know your own body better than anyone else. If you're at the peak of your energy levels early in the day (a morning person), you should do the tasks that require high energy the first thing each day. On the other hand, if you don't hit your stride until later in the day (an evening person), try to match the tasks to your different energy levels. It also helps to do the things you don't care for when you are at your higher energy times. But still focus on getting the high priority items done first. The less important ones can wait.

Some managers divide their lists into three categories: A, B, and C. The A items are the crucial ones that must get done first. If you have several A items, you need to decide which one is the most important and do that one first. The B items can wait until you have the time. The C items are not important. If you never get to do them, it probably would not matter much. Then there are those managers who like to do their C items first because they get a sense of accomplishment. Do not fall into that trap. When you do this, you really are not accomplishing anything. If an A item is too big or foreboding, break it down into a few parts, just as the author in the example did with his writing.

Many people get a psychological lift in drawing a line through the tasks that have been completed. Some of them use a big marking pen. It's great to sit there at the end of the day's activities and see those big marks crossing off so many tasks. It's a feeling of deserved accomplishment.

And don't throw the list away when you leave the office. The next morning, yesterday's list will serve two purposes. It will remind you of all you accomplished the day before—there's nothing wrong with that—and will inform you of what remained unaccomplished. These latter items then go on the new list. That's especially important for long-range projects that might get accidentally dropped from the list. Too many creative ideas and projects get away from us because we didn't write them down.

Have you ever gone to bed with an office problem on your mind, only to wake up in the middle of the night with a solution? Then you awaken in the morning and it's gone. You can't retrieve the idea from your memory. A paper and pen on your nightstand for jotting such thoughts down during the night solves these retrieval problems.

The Closed Period

Some organizations follow a closed-office procedure you may want to use in mapping out your own day to accomplish more. For example, an office will have a two-hour closed period, where it's business as usual except that no one in the office goes to see anyone else. No one makes interoffice phone calls and no company meetings are ever scheduled during this closed period. Genuine emergencies are handled expeditiously; calls from clients, customers, or other outsiders are accepted.

The idea has a great deal of merit. It means you'll have two hours each day when no one from within the company is going to call you on the phone or come into your office. It gives you an opportunity to control what you do during the specified period. Perhaps some person got the idea while working in the office on a weekend and noticing how much more was accomplished than in the same period of time during the week. But the idea is feasible only if you don't shut off your customers or clients during the closed period. It's an idea an entire organization can use to advantage.

The Need for Remembering and Reflecting

Here's a bit of advice that won't do a whole lot for you at the office but will help you remember things you're supposed to stop for on the way home. Put a reminder in the pocket where you keep your car keys. Then, on your way to the parking lot at the end of the workday, you'll reach into your pocket for the car keys and presto!—there it is.

Plan to have a quiet period each day. You may not get it every day, but it's important that you set aside some time for daydreaming and reflection. It's vital to the inner person. Also, problems that seem insurmountable often ease into proper perspective during these quiet times.

And try to put each day's activity into proper context. Here's an idea that, while it may be a bit flaky, gets the concept across. A certain manager kept a one-day calendar next to the door of his office. Beneath it sat a solitary, empty wastebasket. As he left the office at the end of the day, he would tear off the sheet for the day just ending. He stood above the wastebasket and tore that "day" into as many small pieces as he could, then watched the small pieces slowly flutter down into the wastebasket below. When asked what his thoughts were as he went through this ritual, he said, "It symbolizes to me that this day is over. I've done the best I can with it. I now go on to the other segments of my life, leaving this day behind, where it belongs." Not a bad way of letting the completed workday slip into quiet repose.

Other Time Management Tips

Here are some tips recommended by managers from a variety of fields. You may find them helpful as well.

- We all have the same amount of time—168 hours per week. No one has more time than you do. What you do with this time makes the difference.
- It is important to set specific goals for each day or for each week. Do not try to keep these goals in your head. Write them down. Put them on your screensaver or have them written on a bulletin board in your office. Also, read these goals during the day or week. It will be easier to sort out the insignificant work that comes your way.
- Set deadlines for your projects. This especially helps if you are the procrastinator type. Avoid last-minute rush jobs. Some people say they work better under stress and tight deadlines. Perhaps they could work even better if they were not under stress. They need to give it a try.
- Remember the difference between something being urgent versus important. We all have urgent things to do but ask how important they are. It is best to focus on what is important.
- Try keeping a record for a week or two on how you spend your time. Keep a time log and write everything down.

You may be very surprised where a lot of your time is going. If we do not analyze our use of time, we will not be able to manage it better. Or ask others for feedback on how you use your time. They can often see what you cannot.

- Plan your day. The best time to do this is the afternoon or evening before. This way you already know what you are going to be focusing on at the beginning of the next day. If you wait until the morning to do this planning, you may get sidetracked.

- The 70/30 rule: Only schedule about 70 percent of your day. Leave the rest of your time for unplanned assignments, the urgencies of others, or emergencies. If you plan every minute of your day, you will be frustrated when you do not accomplish all of it.

- Schedule set times for sending and returning telephone calls, reading and sending e-mails, office hours, and so forth. This does two things for you. You save time by doing similar items together and you have others eventually learn what your schedule is.

- Make your daily schedule available to anyone who you communicate with on a regular basis. This way they will know where you are and what you are doing. There are many software programs that allow you to do this electronically.

- Realize that interruptions are part of the job and allow time for handling them in your daily schedule. But try to find ways to reduce these unwanted interruptions. Here are a few suggestions: Set up that quiet time so you won't be interrupted. Angle or position your desk so it does not face the traffic flow. When an unexpected visitor comes into your office, stand up and tell them you are working on a key project for the big boss. Remove any chairs from the front of your desk and if you really want someone to stay pull out a chair from behind your desk and invite them to sit down. Or put police tape in your doorway. That quickly gives others the message that you are not to be disturbed.

- Don't wait for that perfect time for you to be in the right mood to work on that high-priority item. That time or mood may never come.

- Reward yourself when you get one of those A priority items completed. Take yourself out to lunch or leave a little earlier that day.

- Develop the on-time habit. Show up on time, hand in things when they are due, and encourage your employees to do the same. Be the model for time mastery in your department.

28

The Written Word

It's a source of amazement and some amusement that many articulate people are reduced to blubbering incompetents when required to put their thoughts down in a written form.

Some people are intimidated by a blank piece of paper or computer screen. Let's examine why this feeling of panic overtakes individuals who otherwise appear to be competent and confident.

First, we have the *test syndrome.* Some people panic when taking examinations. All they have is that blank sheet of paper and the material inside their head, which must be up to translating information to paper. Pass or fail depends on what is scratched on that threatening blank sheet.

A second reason people may not feel confident about using the written word is that they do not read much themselves. They get through what they consider required reading for work, but they don't read for pleasure or for personal or professional development. Instead, they watch too much television, which is more passive than reading. You don't learn much about good writing by watching television. You learn about good writing by reading. Clearly, television is not to be blamed for all the social ills attributed to it. However, few would quarrel that it has lessened the time many people spend reading, which in turn has had an adverse effect on many people's writing skills.

Another reason people panic when they have to write is that they spell poorly and don't want to appear foolish by demonstrating it. So they avoid writing whenever they can, especially if they will have to write ideas or talking points on big sheets of paper or boards in front of others, or even jot down a written note to someone. This avoidance behavior of having to spell seems to be happening more and more. Fortunately, for poor spellers, computers now have spell check. That has saved the day for many of us, at least when we are using a word processing program.

In addition, because people don't write much today, except when they are sending e-mails, they are intimidated when they need to write a lengthy document or even send someone a handwritten letter. An analogy to public speaking might make the point. If you seldom give a speech in public, you are probably intimidated by the situation. And when you are intimidated, you are not relaxed. You are uptight and nervous. Your manner of speaking is stiff and uncomfortable. You communicate your apprehension to the audience; people may even feel uncomfortable for you. Your manner destroys their confidence in you and in the truth or wisdom of the message you are trying to deliver.

The same thing happens with written communication. If you are intimidated by the situation, your writing will be stiff and stilted. Under such circumstances, you may try to cover the situation by writing in a more formal manner, using words you would never use in conversation with a friend.

Books and courses will tell you how to write business letters and interoffice memos. They can be a big help, provided you don't take on the characteristics of the person who wrote the course. Your goal is to improve your technical skills, not to change your personality.

Mental Imagery Helps

One of the best methods for improving your writing skills is to use mental imagery. Instead of being intimidated by the blank piece of paper or screen, get a mental image of the person you are writing to. See that person in your mind. You might even go so far as to imagine the person seated in an easy chair at the office drinking a cup of coffee and reading your note. Or you could visualize yourself sitting in a coffee shop telling the person the message you want to convey.

Imagine that you are having a conversation with the person in a friendly environment. Now speak. Use words you'd use in conversation. If you don't use four-syllable words in your conversations, don't use them in your written communication. Psychologists tell us that people who only use certain words, these fancy types of words, when they want to impress others in their writing are actually showing signs of having an inferiority complex. Even if you do feel uncomfortable with your writing, don't advertise it—keep it to yourself.

When conjuring up the mental picture of the person you're writing to, always imagine a friendly face. Even if you are, for example, sending an e-mail to someone you can't stand, imagine that you're writing to a friend. *Never* conjure up hostile feelings because they may come through in your writing. Imagining a friendly face will bring a friendly, warm tone to your communication.

Now let's take a broader situation: sending an e-mail to all the people in your department or division. You don't want to imagine forty-five people sitting in an auditorium waiting for you to speak. That is too formal a situation, and unless you're an outstanding and relaxed public speaker, the image is going to make your writing formal and uptight.

Instead, get a mental picture of two or three of the friendliest employees you have reporting to you. Imagine that you are on a coffee break or lunch break with them. Now say to them what you have to say. That is what you write. If you're writing to fellow managers in other departments, you can use similar mental images.

Now, let's assume you have to write an update report to the president of the company, and let's assume you are scared to death of Ms. Big. Getting a mental image of the president is only going to make the situation worse. Think instead of someone who does not intimidate you. Imagine that person as the president. Now write the report. The tone will be altogether different.

Writing informally does not mean using incomplete sentences or faulty grammar. Some e-mails sent by educated businesspeople would make their eighth-grade English teachers hide in shame. Companies now offer in-house training courses on how to write proper e-mails. You need to make certain your grammar and spelling are correct.

If you are uncomfortable about your use of grammar or spelling in written communications, learn the basics. They are not that difficult and are certainly not cumbersome. An inexpensive book on grammar and spelling or taking a course at a local college or high school will help you in that regard. Don't rely on an assistant or colleague to backstop you in this area. That is the easy way out and may cause you to put off achieving competence in these important skills.

There is an additional reason you should be sure that your grammar and spelling are correct in your writing. If it isn't, there's a chance that it's also incorrect in your formal speaking and even in informal conversations. If that is the case, it may have an adverse impact on future success and promotion possibilities.

So do your best to write and speak the language correctly and to give it the dignity it deserves. Above all, remember—write to that friendly mental image.

29

The Grapevine

This chapter could be subtitled "The Most Effective Communication." Any organization with more than five people has a grapevine. Grapevines come about because people communicate with each other, and people have a great need to know what is going on. If they don't know, they'll speculate about what is going on. You will never put an end to the grapevine, so you might as well accept its existence and the fact that its tentacles reach into all corners of the organization.

One way a manager can avoid a great deal of incorrect speculation is to do a good job of communication. If you do, they'll have less opportunity to speculate incorrectly about important matters. There will always be speculation and gossip. But by being an effective communicator, you can reduce the *incorrect* speculation. You'll never stop it completely, unless you have the power to impose vows of silence while people are at work, which isn't going to happen.

The grapevine even takes place after hours on the telephone or via e-mail. An example of an e-mail in the evening might go like this: "You didn't get to hear the latest of what's happening now. I heard you were at the dentist. You won't believe this but. . . ." And so it goes on, ad infinitum.

As a new manager you can relate to this story. A few first-time managers working in a commercial bank were wondering how quickly and efficiently the grapevine could handle a rumor. They knew that one of the principal participants was on the fifth floor. They assigned one manager from the group to go to the fifth floor and tell this person an outrageous rumor that could be remotely possible. Then the manager walked back down the stairs to the first floor where his work area was. He was not gone ten minutes. When he got back to his desk, the secretary said, "You'll never believe what I just heard." She repeated the rumor the manager had delivered upstairs, with the addition of a few creative modifications.

Use the Grapevine Sometimes

As a manager you can tap into the grapevine, for both sending and receiving. If you develop good relationships with your people, they'll tell you what is going on. In fact, some of them will vie for the opportunity to be the first to bring you the latest scoop.

You can send messages via the grapevine, too. If you don't use it too often, it can be effective. The emphasis should be on direct communication with your staff, and in doing so, you avoid the embellishments that are invariably tacked on.

If you want to put something into the grapevine as a trial balloon, for example, a perfect opening is "Keep this under your hat, but . . ." or "This is highly confidential, but. . . ." That will ensure its rapid movement through the system. Remember, the only time an item is completely confidential is when you tell no one.

30

Your Best Friend: Delegation

It cannot be stressed enough how important it is for a manager to know how to delegate and to actually delegate. When you delegate properly, you can focus less on performing tasks and more on managing and leading. Delegating is not *doling out*. Delegation is taking something that you currently do and giving it to one of your employees for the purpose of developing their skills. Doling out is saying to an employee, "I am too busy, you have to take some of the workload." Never try to pass off a doling out as a delegation.

Benefits of Delegating

There are many benefits to delegating. You get employees who are more involved and motivated because they are acquitting new skills and developing themselves. Delegation is cost effective for the organization. The company now has someone in-house who can do work that only you were able to do previously. And it frees you up to do other things like manage and lead, take on additional projects from your management, and get in more sets of tennis (just kidding).

Why New Managers Don't Delegate

If delegation is so great, why don't managers do it more often? The number one reason is that they do not know how. It is a skill that needs to be practiced. Then there are the insecure managers. They are afraid that the employee will do it better than they can or they think that their staff will say, "If he is delegating to us, what does he do all day?" And of course, there are those who just love the job so much that they do not want to give it up. None of these are good reasons for not delegating. The only time you should not delegate to others is if someone above you tells you not to or if you have someone who is not ready or is too busy to take on the delegation.

What Should Never Be Delegated

The things that should never ever be delegated even if you are the CEO are all the personnel responsibilities. You always keep performance appraisal, salary reviews, giving positive feedback, coaching, discipline, termination, and so forth for yourself. In addition, if something were of a sensitive or secretive nature like a company downsizing, you would not delegate that task. Have a delegator's consciousness. Try to delegate 100 percent of what you could *possibly* delegate.

Whom to Delegate To

You can really delegate to all your employees. But you have to handle it a little differently depending on whom gets delegated to. And remember, once again, you do not want to overload your best employees because you know they can do it. If you keep overloading them, eventually, they will burn out and you will lose your better performers. When delegating to your less-experienced or less-skilled members, make sure you clearly explain what has to be done and monitor their progress much more than you would one of your more experienced or skilled employees. You can also delegate to the employee who has failed on a previous delegation. When given another opportunity, this employee can regain lost confidence. Try delegating to your problem employees as well. A new challenge or project may cause them to change their outlook on things.

The Delegation Steps

Following is a particular sequence you may find helpful when you delegate. See if this process works for you.

1. Start off by analyzing which of your current tasks, projects, or jobs you could possibly delegate. Think about what goes into getting the job done, how long it takes, what resources are needed, and so forth.

2. Decide whom you could delegate it to. Consider who would be most motivated by the opportunity, who has the time, who either has the skill level or could acquire the skills, and who has asked for additional responsibilities.

3. Once you make up your mind, sit down with the employee and describe as many of the details as possible. Also point out the benefits of taking on the delegation. Obviously, if the person is new or inexperienced, you must spend more time with him or her and provide more details.

4. Finally, discuss how you are going to monitor the employee's progress.

Avoid Upward Delegation

Resist taking on delegations from your direct reports. They will come to you and say they are too busy or the work is too hard or you can do it better than they can. If this happens to you, help them with the project or get a subject matter expert to help them; do not take it over. As manager, you want to be in the business of developing others, not rescuing them.

In The Future

Delegation can be a great friend to you, your team, and the organization. Start thinking about what you could possibly delegate today, tomorrow, or sometime in the future. Learn to delegate and then do it; you won't be sorry.

31

A Sense of Humor

Many new managers take themselves much too seriously. Life is earnest, life is grim, and without a sense of humor, it is deadly. New managers need to learn not to take themselves too seriously and to develop a sense of humor.

One reason many of us take ourselves too seriously is because of the immediacy of the world in which we move. Our daily activities are important to us because they're the ones we know most intimately. Therefore, everything that happens at the office looms large in our lives. We should try to do our jobs to the best of our ability, but once we're sure in our own minds that we have done so, we shouldn't worry about it. The key phrase is *once we're sure in our own minds.* Most of us are our own severest critics.

Of course, the work we do is important. If it were not, no one would part with cold cash in return for our efforts. But we must keep what we do in perspective. It may be important in our office, and it may be important to the people who deal with our office, but it may not seem terribly significant when measured against the history of humankind. When you've had a bad day and all seems lost, remember that a hundred years from now no one will care, so why should you let it ruin your year, month, week—or evening, for that matter? Our jobs are important, but let's keep what we do in perspective.

The English author Horace Walpole (1717–1797) said, "The world is a comedy to those that think, a tragedy to those that feel." It's much easier not to take yourself too seriously if you have a sense of humor. Nearly everyone has some sort of sense of humor. But it is more keenly developed in some people than in others. Even if you feel your sense of humor is weak, you can improve it.

Developing a Sense of Humor

Here's a new flash that provides some hope. Many people who have a reputation for being funny, clever, and humorously creative don't really have any of these characteristics. What they have is a terrific memory and a sense of *appropriateness recall.* They can reach back into their memories quickly and find a humorous line they've heard or read that is appropriate to the situation at hand. They get a reputation for having a sense of humor, and they do have one, but they're not necessarily creative. It's much like the difference between perfect pitch, which some feel a person is born with, and relative pitch, which can be developed and practiced.

So you can develop a sense of humor by reading, by seeing the right kind of humorous movies, and by studying comedy. Watch television personalities who have a reputation for being funny. Watch people who are "ear funny." A cream pie in the face or a pratfall might be "sight funny," but you can't use these gags at the office, and seldom in your social life.

Encouraging Laughter

In addition to developing a sense of humor yourself, as a manger you also need to build a work environment that is fun and where laughter is welcome. If the workplace is a fun and enjoyable place to be, your employees will show up more, work harder, and be more productive. There are many different ways to encourage laughter in your department. Here are a few ideas:

- Start off each meeting with a joke or have one of your employees tell the joke.

- Have a bulletin board devoted to laughter. People can place cartoons or comic strips or jokes on it for their colleagues to look at and read.

- A California manager turned one of the storerooms into a laugh room. He put a VCR in the room and stocked it with tapes of sitcoms and comedians. When he or one of his staff members needed a laugh, they would go into the room, put in a tape for a few minutes, and come out laughing.

You might want to try these methods or find some of your own.

Humor—Not Sarcasm

Achieving a reputation for having a dry sense of humor is acceptable; acquiring a reputation as the office clown is not. Most people can appreciate the difference. Being witty is one thing; being a buffoon is quite another. But one warning: If you have never said anything funny at the office, break into humor on a gradual basis; otherwise someone will want to check the water supply.

Many people mistake sarcasm for wit; some sarcasm can be funny, but there's a twofold problem with being sarcastic. First, you achieve a reputation for being a cynic, which is not a welcome trait in the executive suite. Second, sarcasm is often funny at someone else's expense. You don't want people to think you prey on the weaknesses or idiosyncrasies of others. Also you don't want to offend someone and make an enemy. It's best if your humorous remarks point inward or are neutral in nature. Making fun of yourself or your own foibles makes you a self-deprecating wit, which offends no one. Trading insults with another person can be fun, but it's not a practice for beginners and therefore should be avoided.

Humor, the Tension Reliever

A sense of humor is most valuable when things become hectic and tense. A well-placed humorous remark can relieve the tension. It's like opening a steam valve so that the pressure can escape. It's healthy to see humor in tense situations. Even when it seems inappropriate to make your humorous remark aloud, thinking about it may put a smile on your face and keep you from getting a migraine.

We are surrounded by funny situations every day, but it takes a trained eye to see them. As with the beauty all around us, we don't look for them, and we may not even recognize them when we do see them. With practice, however, you'll begin to see the humor in what goes on all around you.

Finally, there's a compelling reason for not taking this life and ourselves too seriously: None of us is going to get out of it alive anyway.

32

Managing, Participating in, and Leading Meetings

In Chapter 27, mention was made of companies that have closed periods during which office personnel don't phone one another and don't attend meetings. That gives them a certain amount of uninterruptible time each day. Indeed, the productivity of the entire country would be greatly increased if all office meetings of more than two people, in business and government, were banned for one year. Meetings are very expensive. You are taking people away from their work. Always consider what alternatives you have to holding a meeting. If the meeting is just for informational purposes, you can send out an e-mail with attachments, but if you want discussion and decision making to occur, a meeting is necessary. One-way communication does not require a meeting unless the meeting participants never see each other. Then, once in a while, it is nice to bring the group together.

The Cost of a Meeting

Can you justify your meeting in terms of its cost versus the benefits?

Let's say you have a meeting planned for your group of

fifteen including yourself. You want to get their reactions to the new procedures put into place last week and discuss a few other items. You have scheduled two hours for the meeting. Let's calculate the cost of this meeting. Assume the average salary of everyone at the meeting is $60,000. Based on seven working hours, that would make the daily salary about $231 and the per person cost for two hours is $66. We multiply that figure by 15 and get $990. Then add on any room rental fees, costs of snacks and coffee, and so forth. Then some of your attendees may have to travel to your meeting location. That takes them away from their work for even a longer period. Ask yourself the same question we started this section with: "Can you justify your meeting in terms of its cost versus the benefits?" If you can, go forward with it. If you cannot, find some alternative.

Advance Notice

An idea that helps generate a more productive meeting is to send the proposed agenda to meeting participants a few days before the meeting. Going to a meeting unprepared is counterproductive. Many meetings are spur-of-the-moment necessities, but a scheduled meeting should have an agenda.

If you are the only person knowledgeable about what is going to be covered, that might feed your ego but it damages the quality of the meeting. Your agenda should list every topic to be discussed and the time frame for each topic. You must always stick to the time frame so that you can end the meeting on time. Nothing exasperates people more than having meetings go beyond the agreed upon or announced ending time.

It is advisable to have different meeting participants take the lead on different agenda items. This gets them more involved and keeps the pressure off you. You can involve your attendees in another manner. Ask them to contribute suggested items for upcoming meetings. Realize that you are not aware of everything going on around you.

Make sure you begin your meetings on time. You are wasting valuable time and resources when you have people sitting around waiting for the meeting to begin. You never want any of your meeting participants to feel that they are not as important as the people you are waiting for. It also really burns your meeting attendees when you are in the midst of the meeting and a senior manager arrives, so you begin the meeting again for his or her benefit.

Another key thing to remember about agendas is to have the most important items listed and discussed first. You have probably attended too many meetings where they took care of the minor items first, which took up most of the allotted meeting time. Then there is never enough time to cover the really important stuff.

Mistakes Managers Make

Many managers who are new to the meeting process feel obligated to have an opinion on every issue. That isn't necessary. Have an opinion where your motivation is the issue, not the perceived need to speak. It's far better to make a few thoughtful statements than to rattle on about everything. It's preferable to have an executive attending the meeting say, "John is a thoughtful person," as opposed to, "You ask John the time, and he builds you a watch," or "He does rattle on, doesn't he?"

The other extreme of remaining silent during the entire meeting is just as bad. It implies you are intimidated by the situation and that is not an image to create. Even if the situation does intimidate you a bit, never let them see you sweat. Chapter 33, which covers public speaking, will help you in this regard.

Never say anything uncomplimentary in a meeting about anyone on your staff. It will be received as disloyalty on your part. Handle situations, not personalities. Managerial careers have been halted by a manager who trashed an employee in front of a high-ranking executive. This type of behavior says more about you than about the employee.

Some managers view a meeting with higher-ranking executives as a place to display management skills and wares. That is all right if you go about it correctly. However, if you view the meeting as a competition with other managers at your level, your emphasis is wrong. Your goal should be to be a productive, contributing member of the committee, not to show up other managers. Competition is the wrong element to bring to the table.

Another mistake that many managers make is seeing which way the boss is going on an issue, so that their positions are the same. The idea is that their bosses will think more of them if they agree with them, or think as they do. Most bosses immediately spot that game, and the managers may be thought of as spineless. Of course, if you have a point of view that is different from your boss, state it in a diplomatic, reasoned way—but you ought to do that anyway. If everyone agrees with the boss, you don't need the committee.

By the way, many managers lack the courage to take a position different from their boss's. Probably in the vast majority of situations, the courage to state a thought-out position, even if different from the boss's, does more for a career than transparent agreement. There are even executives who deliberately throw out a false position to see which sheep will follow, and then agree with someone who had the courage to state the correct position. (Most executives didn't get to their exalted positions by being stupid.)

Any executive chairing a project or a meeting with members she outranks would do well to hold back disclosing her own position until *after* everyone else has given their thoughts and opinions. Example: The president of a company headed up a corporate reorganization project team consisting of seven people. The president wisely didn't announce her opinions until after she'd called for everyone else's. That approach precluded anyone from playing up to the president, if he or she would have been tempted to do so.

An executive does not need employees or projects team members to play up to him or her. This approach might also teach new managers that it is okay to have a different point of view. Of course, as mentioned earlier in this book, some executives say they don't want yes people, but their actions indicate otherwise. These executives end up with rubber-stamp teams and employees who merely provide cover for the executive, and that is a terrible waste of corporate and managerial time.

Advantages of Being on Project Teams

There are several advantages to being placed on a project team:

- First, someone believes you can make a contribution or you wouldn't have been selected. So make the most of it.
- Second, you may come in contact with managers and executives across a wide spectrum of the organization. These are valuable contacts.
- Third, you may have the opportunity to become involved in decisions that reach beyond your own area of responsibility. This broadens your experience with the organization as a whole.

How to Lead a Meeting

When you become the meeting leader, you should take it as a compliment: Someone sees leadership in you. Don't shy away from such an opportunity.

Some of the best training for leading a meeting is in being exposed to some poorly chaired ones. Most meetings last too long. You can't help but wonder if some folks think sitting around at a meeting beats working. But probably the main reason meetings last too long is that they are poorly planned and inefficiently chaired.

In addition to the earlier suggestion about circulating an agenda in advance, distribute the minutes of the previous meeting. Most everyone then reads the minutes before going to the meeting, and except for a minor correction now and then, approval of the minutes is quickly disposed of. Contrast that with everyone sitting around for fifteen minutes reading the minutes and feeling compelled to nitpick them to death.

Obviously, all agendas show starting times of meetings. It

adds discipline to a meeting if you also show the expected closing time. People tend to stay focused on the subjects at hand if the meeting has an expected adjournment time.

Most meetings are run rather informally. You'll seldom chair a committee that requires you to be an expert parliamentarian. If it does get formal, you'll have to familiarize yourself with *Robert's Rules of Order*. Having this reference available is a good thought, but you'll rarely need it. In all the years you've attended business meetings, you probably can't recall any parliamentarian questions having been raised, except in jest.

The rules of common sense should prevail in leading a meeting. Keep your cool. Don't let anyone press your panic button. Be courteous to all meeting participants. Avoid putting people down. Act as a facilitator, not as a dictator. Keep to the subject. Don't cut people off before they've had their say, but don't allow them to drift away from the subject. Always deal with the problem at hand. A fair meeting leader discourages the same points from being expressed repeatedly.

Don't get involved in personalities, even if others do. Be better organized than anyone else at the meeting. Develop the kind of thoughtful relationships with participants that will prompt them to come to you beforehand with unusual items, thereby avoiding unpleasant surprises. Be fair to everyone, even minority opinions that are unlikely to prevail. The majority view should not steamroll the minority opinion, at least until that opinion has had a fair hearing. If you are fair to all viewpoints, you'll earn the respect of all the participants. Being a successful meeting leader is another chance to display the high quality of your management skills.

Other Meeting Tips

- Establish ground rules at the beginning of a meeting. Ground rules are agreed upon behaviors that everyone follows. They help the meeting run more smoothly and they avoid a lot of disruptive behaviors. Meetings have ground rules about staying on topic, allowing everyone to participate, criticizing the suggestion but not the messenger, and so forth. Ground rules are very helpful and you would be wise to develop a set with your meeting participants.

- Spend five or ten minutes at the end of a meeting to discuss with the group how the meeting went. You want to get feedback so you can improve the quality of the next meeting you run.

- Have on the top of your agenda the purpose of the meeting and what you anticipate achieving.

- Only invite those individuals who should really be there. As a rule of thumb, have the fewest people possible. Also, individuals do not have to stay for the entire meeting. They may only be interested in or need to be there for a couple of the agenda items.

- You want your meetings to be as short as possible. Keep in mind that after about two hours most people's attention span is shot. If your meetings run longer, you need breaks. That can become time consuming and even more costly.

- Prepare a follow-up action plan with action items for the different participants. Make sure everyone gets a copy so each person knows what other people's responsibilities are.

- Finally, get rid of the chairs. If you want to reduce the time of your meetings, make people stand. If you do this, a thirty-minute meeting, for example, can be reduced in half. You will need chairs if meetings run more than twenty minutes or people are not physically able to stand. You may also need something for them to lean on if they need to take notes, or for their portables.

33

Taking Center Stage: The Role of Public Speaking in Your Career

It is amazing that there are so many capable managers who can't handle a public speaking situation. Standing up there on the platform, they come off as the dullest clods imaginable. The impression the audience receives is that they're not very good on the job, either. That impression may not be correct, but as we've discussed earlier, people act based on their perceptions.

Prior Preparation

Many managers are rotten public speakers because they wait until they find themselves in a speaking situation before they do anything about it. By then, it's too late. You can be the greatest manager in the world, but your light will be hidden under a bushel basket if you don't prepare yourself to be a public speaker.

Because so few people in managerial positions prepare themselves to speak publicly, you'll have a leg up on most of them if you learn how it's done. Public speaking frightens many

195

people, and so they avoid it like the plague. Many people—not just managers—have a fear of public speaking. In fact, public speaking ranks near the top of phobias that people have.

As a new manager, you may have the option of not having to do presentations or public speaking to outside groups but you probably will not have that choice within your own organization. It may be a meeting of your department in which you have to get up and explain a new company policy. It may be a retirement dinner for someone in your area of responsibility, and you're expected to make a "few appropriate remarks." You may have to do a client presentation or one in front of the board of directors. Your boss may be out ill and you may have to pitch hit for him or her at the last minute. Managers will often go to unbelievable lengths to avoid these types of speaking situations. They will use ploys such as arranging a business trip so they'll be out of town, or scheduling their own vacation for that time. They'll spend the rest of their business lives plotting how not to get up in front of a group and speak. How much better off they'd be if they'd obtain the necessary skills and turn these negative situations into resounding advantages.

What many people don't realize is that learning to be an excellent public speaker will also improve their ability to speak extemporaneously. How do you respond when you're unexpectedly called on to say a few words? The most extreme example of someone who has difficulty in front of an audience is the person who couldn't lead a group in silent prayer.

Presentation training won't get rid of the butterflies in your stomach, but it will organize them into effective squadrons.

Where to Receive Presentation Training

There are three specific ways that can help you to learn how to be an effective presenter. First, there is Toastmasters International, an organization dedicated to the concept of developing skills in listening, thinking, and speaking. There are neither professionals nor staff members in these clubs, only people who have a mutual interest in developing their speaking capacity. For a modest semiannual fee, you receive the materials you'll need to begin the process. You go at your own speed, and you'll find a group of people who help one another not only by providing an audience but also by engaging in formal evaluation sessions.

Another aspect of the Toastmasters' training that is invaluable is what are called Table Topics. This part of the meeting is designed to develop your skills in extemporaneous speaking. The Topic Master calls on various people (usually those not scheduled to give a formal speech that evening) to talk for two or three minutes on a surprise subject. The time you have to prepare extends from the moment you rise from your chair until the moment you arrive at the lectern.

There are Toastmasters clubs all over the world, so it's likely that you'll find one in your area. If not, you can go online to www.toastmasters.org.

The next way to build up your public speaking ability is to take a training course or a college course in presentation skills. There are many training organizations available that offer excellent programs. One of them is the American Management Association (AMA). The organization has programs throughout the world. Its Web site is www.amanet.org. Both Toastmasters and AMA are nonprofit organizations.

The third way to become an effective presenter is to get one-on-one coaching. Here, you or your company hires an individual to give you private instruction and guidance. It is expensive but really worth it. Your HR department can help you locate a qualified individual.

By no means are these three suggestions your only alternatives. You can read books, watch professionals in action, find someone in-house whose presentations you admire and ask them to work with you, or rent videos or tapes on the topic.

Next Week's Presentation

You might be saying to yourself that these are all great suggestions for the future, but what do you do if you have to give a presentation next week. Here are some basic things to remember and do when presenting in front of a large group:

• *Decide what the purpose of your presentation is and write it out in one sentence.* It should not be longer than one sentence and should be clear to anyone listening to it or reading it. Also think of your purpose in behavioral goals. That is, what do you want the audience to get from your presentation? Do you want them to remember certain things, know a particular procedure, or physically be able to demonstrate the use of something?

• *Develop your subject matter outline.* Most studies have shown audiences only remember one main point and three subpoints. Keep the presentation as brief and tight as possible.

• *During the planning for and delivery of the presentation, keep these well-known words about presentations in mind: "Tell them what you are going to tell them (do this in the opening), tell them (do this in the main body of your talk), then tell them what you told them (do this in your conclusion)."*

• *Before planning your talk try to do an audience analysis.* Find out who they are, their reasons for being there, their interest and academic levels, their attitudes, their cultural backgrounds, ages, and so forth. The more you know in advance about the audience, the better you will be able to prepare for your talk.

• *During the presentation watch your audience.* Are they smiling and attentive or restless, confused, engaging in chats with their neighbors, or leaving? You may need to change your delivery style by talking louder or lower, faster or slower, cut things short or explain in more depth, change your tone of voice, and so forth.

• *If you are using visuals like PowerPoint slides, don't talk to the slides, talk to the audience.* Most new managers make this mistake. Visuals should be a backup for the audience. You need to be the main attraction.

• *Practice, practice, practice.* If you are prepared and comfortable with what you are presenting, you will come across as much more relaxed and you will experience much less stage fright. However, do not make the mistake of memorizing your presentation. This can be disastrous if you forget your place.

• *Be ready to adapt to all situations.* You never know what might happen at a presentation. The equipment may be faulty, rendering useless your wonderful slides or video clips. You have to be ready to quickly reorganize your presentation. Or suppose your plan includes having the audience break up into small groups for discussion purposes during your presentation. But the auditorium has those chairs that cannot be moved. You've got to have an alternative plan or your presentation will fall apart before you begin.

• *Be energetic, lively, and demonstrate to the audience that you are enjoying your talk.* If you don't, you really should not expect them to be enthusiastic and interested.

Fringe Benefits

How many outstanding public speakers do you personally know, either inside or outside your organization? Probably not many, if any. Why don't you resolve to be one of the few who are outstanding? Think of the possibilities not only for promotion within your company but also for positions of leadership within the community. As a matter of fact, the opportunities for leadership challenges may come more quickly outside the company. Consider what that may open up for you. There are many followers out there waiting for someone to lead them. One characteristic most outstanding leaders have is the ability to speak persuasively on public occasions. There is no reason why you can't be one of those few leaders.

PART SIX

THE COMPLETE PERSON

34

Coping with Stress

Many new managers believe they should be able to arrange their work life so that there will be no stress. But stress cannot be avoided. Occasionally, it will come calling. How you react to it is the key. You cannot always control what happens; what you can control is how you react to what happens to you.

What causes work-related stress?

There are innumerable causes for work-related stress. We all have different thresholds to what is stressful for us. But anything that takes our body or mind out of whack is stressful. Here are some typical work-related stressors:

- Receiving no direction from the boss
- Computer failures
- Constant interruptions
- Priorities constantly changing
- Upper management constantly changing
- Mergers
- Downsizing
- Reorganizations
- Organizational politics
- Time pressures

- Performance pressures
- Poor time management
- Bringing personal problems to work
- Working long hours for extended periods of time

No doubt you can relate to many of these stressors.

Some Relief

Here is an interesting factor about stress that may make you feel better about the stress you feel early in your managerial career: Most of what seems stressful when you're new in management will seem ordinary and even mundane after you're experienced. This possibility reinforces the point that it may be your reaction and inexperience that causes you to consider it stress, rather than the situation itself. That may be a fine point, but the distinction seems significant.

Go back in your memory to the days you were taking driver education to learn how to safely operate an automobile. The first time you got behind the wheel was quite stressful. With experience, your ability to drive improved to the point that driving now seems as natural as brushing your teeth. The situation has not changed, but your experience and reaction to it has changed.

How you react to apparent stressful situations is part of your management style. Too many managers look so deep in thought. The brow is furrowed all the time. This demeanor is contagious to everyone working with you; unfortunately, it's contagious in a most negative way. However, a manager who can smile and be pleasant in what seems to be a stressful situation instills confidence in all who are working on the project.

It's hard to think clearly when you are uptight and nervous, so that reaction exacerbates the situation. That is a double whammy. You have a stressful situation, and your reaction diminishes your ability to bring it to a successful resolution.

The third whammy is the knowledge that says, "I'm going to be judged by how I handle this type of situation." That element adds even more pressure. Telling yourself not to get uptight is like someone telling you not to worry. It's much easier said than done.

There are those who believe that stressful situations get the juices flowing and bring out the best in people. You've heard the old saw, "When the going gets tough, the tough get going." That is true once you get over the fear of a stressful situation. Fear is like pouring the juices of stress down through a very small funnel.

React to the Problem, Not the Stress

To succeed, you must convert the fear of a stressful situation into the challenge of a stressful situation. If you are going to be a manager who periodically faces stressful situations, here are seven suggestions for you:

1. Don't be panicked into impulsive action. It may make matters worse.

2. Take several deep breaths and try to relax. Speak slowly, even if you don't feel like it. This instills calm in those around you. It says, "He's not losing his head, and therefore I shouldn't."

3. Reduce the situations to two or three key points that could be handled to remove the urgency of the moment, so that the rest of it can be processed in a nonurgent way.

4. Assign three or four major elements to members of the staff to process in parts and then be combined into the whole.

5. Ask for suggestions and ideas from the experienced members of your staff.

6. Think about the problem and not your reaction to it.

7. View yourself as an actor playing the role of the wise, calm, and decisive leader. Play that role to the hilt, and after a while it will cease to be role-playing and will be you. This constitutes changing your reaction to the stressful situation.

Have Confidence in Your Abilities

As a manager, you handle tougher questions than those that came to you before the promotion. If they were all easy, anyone could solve them. You are there because someone saw in you the ability to deal with these more difficult situations. As you move up the corporate ladder, the problems become more complex, or so it seems. The important thing to remember is that your experience will remove most of the stress. When you've been a manager for a while, you will not react the same way to the same situation, as you did the first few months in your managerial career. *It will get better.*

In the early days in management, just having the job brings elements of stress. That is why so many new managers look intense, as though they are carrying the weight of the world. While the concern and the desire to perform well are commendable, the intensity gets in the way of getting the job done. You are managing people in the tasks they need to complete in order to achieve a desired result. You are not leading them out of the trenches, with bayonets at the ready, across a minefield to engage the enemy in hand-to-hand combat.

The best advice for you to follow as a new manager is "Lighten up."

35

Having Balance
in Your Life

The first-time manager becomes so engrossed in the new responsibilities that the job occupies almost every waking moment. This dedication is admirable, because it indicates that the person is determined to do a great job and be successful as a member of the management team.

But life must have balance. While your career is important, it is not your entire life. Actually, you will be a more complete manager if you are a more complete person. You cannot separate the two.

When you ask people what they do, they will automatically tell you what they do for a living. They are a dentist, accountant, lawyer, salesperson, manager, barber, or trucker. But we are all so much more than what we do to earn our daily bread—or if we're not, we should be.

There are many sad stories of people who retire and lose their sense of identity and sense of worth. The job was their life, and when they retire, they lose their identity. A person who has this reaction to retirement is not a complete person. Their interests, other than their families, all revolve around their careers. It's understandable to miss your work, especially if you enjoyed it, but no longer working should never be the end of all meaningful life.

A person whose only interest is the job is a one-dimensional individual, and a one-dimensional person is not as effective a manager as a multidimensional person.

I'm not referring to your first few months on the job. But after you have successfully passed through the breaking-in period, you need to broaden your interests and your activities.

Community Work

Everyone who aspires to management needs to be involved in the community. You don't take from a community and not put something of yourself back into it. The same is true of your profession. Put something back into your professional associations. These are not completely altruistic recommendations. The primary objective is to be of assistance to the cause of the profession, but there are ancillary benefits. You become known within your community and your profession. You enhance your base of knowledge, and you make some nice contacts and friends. That not only makes you a broader-based manager but also a more promotable one. And the higher you go in the organization, the more important leadership becomes. Community and professional association leadership are viewed most favorably in the executive suite of an overwhelming number of companies.

There have been countless situations where two people being considered for promotion were both qualified as far as the work was concerned. It was a close call, and the difference came down to leadership within and *outside* the halls of the company. In many companies today, staff is allowed "release time" to engage in company sanctioned community service programs.

Outside Reading

While it is vital that you read about your business, it is also important that the manager be a well-read person. A manager should be a well-informed citizen and should know what is going on in his or her city, state, and nation. That means keeping up-to-date by reading newspapers, news magazines, and the trade magazines of your industry. A manager needs to be well informed about the world. What is going on in the world does affect your organization.

It also helps to read a good novel once in a while. Good fiction writers often have great insight into the human condition. Besides, these books are entertaining, and that is positive too. Some managers have their teams read the same book and then the book is discussed at a meeting or get-together. The book can be on leadership, communication, or a subject related to their business. This practice makes for great discoveries about each of the team members and helps build a high-performing team.

All people at all stages of their lives need to stay mentally challenged and alert. It's much easier to do that if you maintain broad-based interests. Reading is just one way to do that.

Leave Work Behind

You must have the ability and determination to separate work from the rest of the day. It is important to be able to leave work at work and go on with the rest of your life. We need to have interests, hobbies, and other things to do outside of work. That really helps us give our life balance. A big mistake made by many managers, especially new ones, is to take work home with them. Most managers who do this never get to it. And it adds to their stress levels, because they think about the work all night or all weekend and see it every time they pass it sitting there on the dining room table. Stop taking work home. Either stay a couple extra hours at work that day or show up early the next day or on Monday morning.

36

A Touch of Class

There are many meanings to the word *class*. The meaning we will concern ourselves with is "style and elegance in one's behavior." Class in a manager or executive consists of what is done and, often of greater importance, what is *not done*.

- Class is treating people with the dignity their humanity deserves. It is not in treating them as objects of production.

- Class has nothing to do with your social status in life. It has everything to do with your behavior.

- Class does not use foul language, even when irritated. Class means having the large vocabulary that makes four-letter words unnecessary.

- Class does not have to be the center of attention. It can allow others to bask in glory without feeling slighted.

- Class does not tell off-color or racially demeaning jokes.

- Class separates any sexual desires from the workplace, and would never make a remark to a person of the opposite sex that wouldn't be said in front of one's mother, if she were standing alongside.

- Class does not say anything derogatory about the organization, no matter how justified you may feel it is, at a moment of disappointment.

- Class does not allow the unsatisfactory actions or negative words of others to drag one down into that ugly arena.
- Class does not lose its cool. It never burns its bridges.
- Class does not rationalize mistakes. It learns from them and moves on.
- Class in a manager emphasizes *we* and downplays *I.*
- Class is good manners.
- Class means respect for oneself as a foundation for respect for others.
- Class never makes a demeaning remark about one's spouse. These remarks say more about the speaker than the spouse.
- Class in a manager means loyalty to one's staff.
- Class means not believing one is superior to one's employees; each simply has different responsibilities.
- Class does not take action when angry. It waits until cool reason has returned. Class is not impetuous.
- Class recognizes that the best way to build oneself is to first build others.
- Class does not become overly concerned about receiving credit. Class also recognizes that sometimes one receives more credit than one deserves. It helps balance out those times when there are no accolades.
- Class works hard at making action consistent with words.
- Class doesn't build oneself up by tearing others down.
- Class leads by example.
- Class knows the importance and value of a warm smile.

Conclusion

A variety of topics have been covered in this book on how to lead people, but certainly not every situation you'll confront in your career as a manager—or even within the first few weeks in your new role—has been reviewed.

There is no way that a book of this sort can be made all-inclusive. It is the hope that you have gained some insight into the techniques of managing people that will make the job more meaningful, enjoyable, and understandable. You may think that we've spent an inordinate amount of time on attitudes, on how you view yourself and the problems you face, but that is exactly where your success or failure in working with people will be determined—in your head.

If you're the type of person who believes you're primarily controlled by events, then what's the use? You're merely a puppet then, with some giant puppet master pulling the strings. But in actuality, it's not that way. Although events beyond your control do have an impact on your life, you control how and what you think. That in turn controls your reaction to these events.

There has been no conning in this book. You haven't been told that if you work hard and keep your nose clean you'll rise to the top. However, you'll have a better chance if you follow some of these concepts than if you ignore what are basic truths.

You didn't come into this world with any guarantee that everything would be fair and that the deserving would always get what they deserve. They don't! However, you obviously have no chance to achieve your goals if you just sit there and wait for lightning to strike.

We must grow. This book is devoted to exploring how you manage your people, but equally important is seeing you grow as a total person. Your career can add to your total growth, since it's such a large part of your life. We shouldn't work at a job we don't like, but on the other hand, we must be realistic in recognizing that all careers contain aspects we don't like. It's the balance that is important. If most of the job is enjoyable, satisfying, and challenging, then you can put up with the few parts you don't care for. If it's the other way around and you dislike most of what you have to do, you're obviously in the wrong career and you ought to change it. Life is too short to spend time and energy in a career that destroys you.

You have known people who stick with a job they don't like because someday it will provide a great retirement benefit. What good does that prospective retirement benefit do if people ruin their health before they get to retirement? What's worse, they might not live that long.

There are also people who complain about a job constantly but never seek a better job because their fear of change or the unknown is more powerful than their dislike of the job. Some people prefer the predictable (even if it's bad) over something new or unknown.

Perhaps Abraham Lincoln was right when he said, "Most people are about as happy as they make up their minds to be." That summarizes what this book has addressed about the primacy of attitudes.

Too many people, as they approach their middle years, start thinking in terms of the kind of contribution they're making to the world. They often become depressed because they believe what they're doing is not very important. They ask themselves, "How significant is it that I'm a manager in a company making bolts?" Put in that context, it may not seem terribly relevant. But the question that should be asked is, "What kind of impact am I having on the people I come in contact with, both in my work and in my personal life?"

If you can answer that question in a positive way, it doesn't matter whether the company you're associated with is making bolts or life-saving medicine. The system isn't the payoff; the product isn't the payoff; your impact on the people whose lives you touch is what is important. Also, holding a position that is a little higher on the organization chart *does not* make you more important than they are. An executive or a manager is a combination of leader and servant. Not many executives are willing to accept the servant aspect of their responsibilities, because it interferes with their exalted opinion of their rank.

In developing systems for your people to use, you're in fact serving them. In maintaining a salary administration and performance appraisal system, you're serving them. In working out vacation schedules that allow your people to maximize the benefits of their relaxation time, you're serving them. In hiring and training quality people for your department, you're serving the people who are already there.

Most people have no difficulty understanding the proposition that the president of the United States has immense power but is also a servant—in fact, the number one public servant. The same concept applies to managerial jobs. There is a combination of what appear to be contradictory concepts: authority and a responsibility to serve. If you can keep these in some semblance of balance, you'll avoid getting an inflated view of your own importance. You'll also do a better job.

You don't necessarily get smarter. You gain more experience, which many people mistake for wisdom. It doesn't matter what you call it as long as you continually become more effective. You become more effective as you develop a greater variety of experiences in working with people. You gain little from repeating the same experiences except a smoothness that might not otherwise develop.

And the point, although elementary, bears repetition: There is a great deal to be gained from developing empathy for your employees' attitudes and feelings. Can you really sense how you'd want to be treated if you were in their position?

The best of success to you as you direct people in what

amounts to nearly one-half of their waking hours. Your success as a manager starts with you and your attitude toward that responsibility. It is hoped that this book has been of help to you at the beginning of a new and exciting chapter in your life. Good luck to you and enjoy the ride.

Index